SWAT
Mentality

D1547657

JEFF TANNER

ISBN 978-1-64670-259-6 (Paperback)
ISBN 978-1-64670-260-2 (Digital)

Copyright © 2020 Jeff Tanner
All rights reserved
First Edition

Cover design by Joseph Dykeman, Average Joe Solutions

All rights reserved. No part of this publication may be reproduced, distributed, or transmitted in any form or by any means, including photocopying, recording, or other electronic or mechanical methods without the prior written permission of the publisher. For permission requests, solicit the publisher via the address below.

Covenant Books, Inc.
11661 Hwy 707
Murrells Inlet, SC 29576
www.covenantbooks.com

I wish to dedicate this book to all those fellow team members of the Pasco Sheriff's Office SWAT Team who served alongside me during my years on the team. I am forever indebted to those mentors who taught me so much during my early years on the team, and all team members who served faithfully alongside me in the resolution of so many search warrants, barricades, hostage situations, etc. I am truly grateful to those who stepped up to pursue membership on our team during my tenure, to acquire the knowledge, skills and attitude to resolve high risk situations, and continue the high standards of professionalism for our team. In John 15:13, it is stated, "Greater love has no man than this, than to lay down one's life for his friends." While we were always ready to make such a sacrifice, in the furtherance of the pursuit of truth and justice for our county's citizens, I am thankful no team member ever had to make the ultimate sacrifice. I pray your Christian walks take you closer and closer to Jesus, and the peace that only Jesus can bring to you.

CONTENTS

Introduction...7

Chapter 1: The Early Years.....................................11

Chapter 2: The Rifle Club 19

Chapter 3: What Do I Want to Be When I Grow Up? 23

Chapter 4: The Rookie Deputy................................26

Chapter 5: Striving for the Goal.............................32

Chapter 6: Qualification Time...............................37

Chapter 7: My First Barricaded Subject SWAT Callout............42

Chapter 8: The Major Search Warrant in Blanton.....................46

Chapter 9: Move Out, Move Out, Move Out 53

Chapter 10: Barricaded Man in a Van 59

Chapter 11: Tryouts for the Sniper Team 72

Chapter 12: Chester's Last Stand.................................76

Chapter 13: The Following Years 90

INTRODUCTION

As I take a pen in hand to begin these short stories, I wish to take a moment to introduce myself, as well as lay out the background of this personal history of the development of my SWAT mentality over the course of my lifetime.

First, I'd like to thank you for taking the time to explore some of my personal experiences, exploits, and life lessons which were so critical to the development of my own SWAT mentality prior to and during my SWAT years. My only wish for your takeaway of these stories is to open your own personal perspective of the all-important investment that is required for a SWAT dude, the commitment, and level of sacrifice which is so important for each and every member of a high-risk response team. As you discover this aspect of a SWAT member, you will likely make your own comparison of where you take on a SWAT mentality in your own life. Somewhere, somehow, you may view a given aspect of your life with certain tactical precision and analysis. You may have a specific driving route which you follow during your daily commute or drive to your children's daycare center. You may have a specific tactic which works best for you to avoid the crowd as you enter a local government building to get to your office quickly and without interruption so as to land you in your desk chair by 8:00 a.m. each and every day. Only you know what traits and practices which give you that little advantage in life to put you ahead of the competition, the herd, the masses, and give you that special pleasure to know you are set just slightly above the rest of the people.

Now when you look at that from a SWAT perspective, we use dedicated phrases to refer to the advantages that we enjoy. Those little tactical advantages can take on much meaning over time, especially when they give us so much cumulative boost in our lives and spirit.

Through the course of this book, I will mention many of the phrases in key areas, which have taken on special meaning for me and many other SWAT guys whom I have had the pleasure of serving with over many years. The importance of these phrases is evident when you realize how they lift our mentality to a degree and give us the reason for pushing onward for superiority in our lives, in our battles, and in our families.

Please understand the strong degree of faith which any SWAT dude must have in the Father, Son, and the Holy Spirit, which is critical to survive in today's hostile world. As society has changed over the past several years, the decrease in respect for our first responders, public servants, and protectors has been much more apparent. I've seen less compassion and consideration for the loyalty, dedication, and commitment of our law enforcement and those who are known as the "sheepdogs of our society."

If you don't quite understand that concept, I would encourage you to explore the expert in the field, Lieutenant Col. (retired) Dave Grossman. He describes the concept of all of society is composed of sheep, who blindly go about their daily routines, grazing contentedly, just hanging out with the other sheep, until the wolf comes knocking at the door. The wolf represents the "bad man" of society, and the wolf preys upon the weak and helpless without mercy, the sheep. However, the wolf doesn't always get his way as the sheep are protected by the sheepdog. The sheepdog is ever vigilant, watching over the sheep and keeping them safe throughout the day and the night.

The funny thing is, nobody likes the sheepdog, and he is not like the other sheep. He is different and follows a different school of thought; to watch over the sheep takes a special type of sheepdog. So the sheepdog watches until the wolf comes knocking at the door. At which time, he steps into action to protect whoever he must and at great personal risk. Yet despite this commitment to protecting the sheep, the sheepdog is still not liked by the sheep society, but that does not matter as he does what he does for the benefit of the many, for the minimizing of the risk of loss to the few.

So whether a law enforcement agency wishes to call their specialty team a SWAT team, TAAT team (Tactical Assault and Apprehension Team), ERT (Emergency Response Team), TLT (Tactical Lifesaving

Team), etc., or any other version of many alphabet soup acronyms, the important thing is, most or all members of that team have a committed sense of responsibility to the sacredness of life, the ties that bind a family together, and the God-given opportunities to live our lives freely and expressly how we choose, according to human will and with the blessings of our Lord and Savior.

Although this book is not written directly as an inspirational Christian series of stories, many of you will note the undeniable touches of God's grace throughout the trials, comedies, and confusion. It is inevitable, but I would shudder to think of the outcome if His hand had not been present throughout many of these experiences. I will be forever grateful that throughout the many conflicts which our team faced, we were so obviously graced with His guidance, wisdom, and strength. As the scholar Paul said in Philippians 4:13, "I can do all things through Christ who strengthens me."

I do hope you realize as I learned very early in my law enforcement career, we police and SWAT dudes are granted a very expansive, somewhat intrusive perspective into the private lives of your families, friends, and neighbors. Many of these people would not respond kindly to the exposure of the moments of their lives (private moments), which they would much rather keep hidden in the past. So as each segment unfolds, without sacrificing the details or accuracy of each story, most identifiable elements, names, and specific locations have been changed or deleted. Hopefully this will offer a layer of protection to protect the personal connection of those stories which some members would rather not have exposed to the public.

For those who may see some elements which they recognize, albeit a part of their own lives or experience, I only request you share with me whatever lessons you learned or laughs that you took away from the incidents. Please, above all, I ask you to understand the commitment of our first responders who, every day, put their heart and soul into their service above self to others with the self-sacrifice for the love of fellow man. After all, that is all we have to give during our time on earth, which shows our Heavenly Father how much we praise Him, love Him, and thank Him for giving us this time on His beautiful earth.

Chapter 1
The Early Years

Before I formed you in the womb, I knew you
before you were born, I set you apart.
—Jeremiah 1:5

My name is Jeff Tanner, and I grew up in a normal family just like most people you and I know. I was born in an average, industrial town nestled in the foothills of the Allegheny Mountains of western New York. I learned early on in my life how much fun the winter snow could be for me and my brothers as we watched the plentiful blizzards which blew in across the frozen waves of Lake Erie to cover the frozen landscapes with fluffy white covering, just begging us to grab our sleds, snowboards, silver saucers, or whatever else we could grab in a hurry and fling ourselves down the nearest hill.

We spent day after day building snowmen, sledding down any hill in the neighborhood, and even ice-skating on the largest local freshwater lake, where I later learned to swim when the summer sun finally warmed up the lake to a bearable temperature. Although bearable temperature was a figure of speech, when you've been practicing your kicking technique for thirty minutes, and the swim teacher pulls you out of the water for fifteen minutes to warm up in the sunny part of the waterside grass, wrapped in a thick warm towel, I felt the hardest part of swimming lessons was staying in the water long enough to practice.

This same lake, Chautauqua Lake, was famous among freshwater fishermen, both in summer or winter, for delivering on their hopes of catching a nice size bass, muskie, or walleye, which seemed to even bring the tourists into our community to give it a try. Although the experience of venturing out onto the rough icy terrain with a drill to make a hole in the ice was not my favorite means of dropping some bait into the water for the benefit of any swimming creature to nibble upon for their personal survival.

Our days in western New York were only for the first ten years of my lifetime, as the Lord had other plans for our family and those did not involve staying in the Lake Erie winter wonderland for the duration of my school-aged years. So after my father received his draft notice to help offer whatever help he could for the cause of the Vietnam War, we were allowed to wait 'til my mother gave birth to my youngest brother, and then we moved to Louisiana. Thank you to the US army for the opportunity to postpone our pending move so she could give birth in a local hospital outside of Buffalo surrounded by family support.

Upon moving to the deep south in the heat of August, my brothers and I found ourselves exploring a very different kind of playground. This was well into the era of the Vietnam War (1971) with troops actively training on military bases throughout the military training facilities all through the United States. As they suffered bumps, bruises, strains, and sprains, someone needed to bandage them up and tend to them. Someone needed to X-ray their muscle tears, broken bones, and bumps on their heads. That was my dad, who never thought his draft number would come up to be told, "Uncle Sam, needs you!" But nevertheless it did, and just two weeks after my third brother was born, we found ourselves living on a southern army base several miles from the Texas or Louisiana border.

We were welcomed to Leesville, Louisiana, and the Army Basic Training base known as Fort Polk (named after President James K. Polk). We surmised based on the state of Fort Polk's condition; this base had not seen much renovation or improvement since President James K. Polk's first term as President of our great United States.

Three very different but still relevant watershed moments occurred during this time of my life, which will provide more significance later in this story and in relation to the development of my SWAT mentality. While adapting to life as a new "military" family, our initial available housing was on the base itself. A very basic, wood-framed, generic, and nondescript "cottage" house became our new home. The cottage was built up on concrete blocks, slightly elevated, and painted a faded yet drab yellow color, which must have been available at a huge cost savings to the military. We reached this conclusion because almost every building in the immediate vicinity of our base housing was painted the same ugly faded shade of yellow.

So why didn't the military use bright, cheerful colors to paint the new homes for new military families? Well, the answer is quite simple as we soon found out. Since the military is a branch of government, and government runs on tax dollars, the definition of tax dollars would designate a finite number rather than an infinite number. So to make that huge bulk purchase of drab yellow paint go as far as possible, they painted *everything* with it. And I do mean everything!

Point taken…all of government runs on a very tight budget. Good to know!

As the days progressed, my brothers and I ventured farther and farther onto the grounds around our new on-base home and found Fort Polk held many interesting things that my ten-year-old mind struggled to sort into the proper categories and life lessons for future reference. For instance, picture a huge sandy field, kind of like a bunch of football fields, with the occasional patch of grass. This was deep south territory, so the ground was covered more with sand than dirt, and the wooded areas were covered more with pines and palms than oaks or maples. Anyway, in various areas of this playground for men (as women in combat roles were still a very taboo idea at this time), there were rows of obstacles that fit the profiles of humans, anchored solidly in the sandy ground, constructed of car tires, which had long ago outlived their usefulness but had been retired to this strange course that could have just as easily been labeled the killing fields. When the squads and platoons of soldiers were brought out to these killing fields, they carried the same identical rifles that I would later learn to identify as a Colt M16, and they were issued to every soldier drafted or enlisted in this lengthy battle against communism in a little Asian country called Vietnam.

The sergeants or platoon leaders would bark out their orders as the soldiers would slowly navigate through the rows of planted rubber adversaries while violently but methodically placing the bayonet of their rifle deep into the "body" of each rubber enemy soldier, only to yank the bayonet out of the enemy, step around the figure, and advance to the next one. Every bad man on the field got served, and God help the poor exhausted soldier who tried to move past a rubber man without serving up a good healthy dose of twelve inches of tempered steel to the gut.

The sergeants yelled in his ear for a good five minutes straight while that soldier got to show how many push-ups he could do while the sergeant swore and told the soldier how badly he had messed up. Then the soldier got to demonstrate in his best soldierly way how to attack the next rubber enemy until the sergeant told him it was safe to proceed to the next rubber man.

Point taken...if you let a bad man live in a violent confrontation, he will inevitably kill you and all your buddies on your team before you can move on. Good to know!

Remember, this is my ten-year-old mind trying to wrap around these new concepts of training for war. And this was long before I had ever been exposed to SWAT training concepts, Biblical conflicts, or Sun Tzu and *The Art of War*. And as far as exposure to Christian faith, I had attended a Methodist church with Sunday school activities for five years from the age of three to eight. And since arrival in Leesville and Fort Polk, I had begun attending another Bible study class with a neighboring military family who introduced me and my brothers to a Baptist church service. So my understanding and knowledge of wars and conflicts in the Biblical times was rather familiar and intact. After all, I could sing you the entire song about Joshua won the battle at Jericho.

Second awakening for ten-year-old Jeff while living on (or near) Fort Polk came one day when I was in the front seat of my dad's car. We were driving through the base when a long caravan of big troop transport trucks appeared in front of us. My dad instinctively slowed down to let the trucks go before us, and one by one they revved their deep, guttural diesel engines roaring across the intersections toward the huge airfield at the north side of the base. These soldiers bouncing around in the back of the trucks seemed to be much more fully dressed out for battle with all kinds of gear, rifles slung on their backs, and big packs on the floor between the rows of green army men seated facing toward each other.

So being the curious one, heretofore only seeing army men training with the green-camouflage pants and dark-green T-shirts, and only previously having seen the big bulky packs carried on their backs while marching through the base, I had to know what made these army men special in that they got the obvious "privilege" of riding in the back of these huge trucks, instead of trotting "double-time" across the base.

"Dad," I said. "How come those guys are wearing different-looking uniforms in the back of those trucks?"

"Well," he said. "They're done with basic training, and now they're shipping out."

"Oh!" This seemed to open up a myriad of further questions, but I did my best to pick just one so I didn't get on his nerves. I kept it short again. "Where are they going?"

He answered with a solemn tone that seemed as though it hung forever in the humid Louisiana afternoon air. "Vietnam."

Yes, I had heard about Vietnam as my mother and dad had discussed it many times when we lived in New York before Jimmy (my youngest brother) was even born. Until then, the draft was just a blast of cool air that happened to find you when you were trying to stay warm in the cold western New York winters. Now I knew that once drafted, the soldiers were sent to army bases, put through all kinds of training in how to fight and kill people, shoot their M16 rifles, swim in a huge pool (where I took swimming lessons), and even march across the entire army base. They were trained in how to run for long distances without getting tired and how to run through the woods, going over, under, and through these big log obstacles, climbing or swinging on ropes, climbing cargo nets, balancing on big logs set end to end, and even climbing a big wood tree house so they could slide down a long rope from the top. The rope slide took them all the way to the ground again so they could run all the way back to the starting point.

Someone had even gone to the trouble of engraving names for each obstacle on a plaque, so as the soldiers ran up to each new obstacle, they could see what they were about to conquer, like "balance logs" or "belly buster" or "high rope slide." I kind of thought that if the soldier wanted to see what obstacle was next, all he had to do was look at it. But then I learned that each obstacle had a different, more descriptive name too, though these were much more interesting. They seemed to be much more animated too, depending on how the soldiers had injured themselves as they tried to go through each obstacle event.

So after all this training, then came the real-life application of all those training concepts in a live fire environment. And that was how I learned that soldiers were not just intuitively born as soldiers but had to undergo extensive training and preparation before they even set foot on a battlefield. But because our country was fighting this war, each soldier had to be prepared for whatever they might encounter while over in Vietnam, especially when they were fighting in hot, humid weather conditions. So an Army base like Fort Polk was considered very important for training these soldiers because they were exposed to the hot and humid training environment to better prepare them for Vietnam.

Point taken…after the training, comes the violent confrontation. If the training was good preparation (factoring in lots of other variables), the good guy will live and emerge victorious like the story of David and Goliath.

Later on, I had the good fortune to advance to a position as SWAT team commander, under a sheriff who put his faith and trust in my abilities to lead our team into the training and preparation for whatever barricaded subjects, hostage situations, search warrants, and dignitary protection details we might have to encounter. I was invited to participate in a radio show interview hosted by the press relations person of our agency. During this interview, while trying to present SWAT concepts to the general public in a broadcast radio show, I had the not so fortunate opportunity to proclaim a SWAT adage which summed up this process. I told them (the public), "The more we sweat in time of peace, the less we bleed in time of war."

This seemed to summarize the extensive training and preparation which our SWAT team prided itself upon as we spent a whole eight hours of training time every month, about ninety-six hours per year, plus a few extra weeks in training classes throughout each year to keep our SWAT skills as sharp as we could keep them in preparation for the many violent encounters during the course of each year.

Albeit this was an accurate phrase for the reality of SWAT training; however, when the sheriff heard these words come out of my mouth, he distinctly heard me refer to the night-and-day juxtaposition of war and peace right here in our "bedroom community" of Tampa Bay, where he wished for our citizens to feel nothing more than warm and safe and cozy every day and night. He also heard me refer to SWAT guys as sweating as we so often did during the training sessions, and then he heard the reference to SWAT guys bleeding as well. I can only imagine his image of the level of violence in our cozy community that would cause our SWAT team members to bleed all over, and if the situations were so bad for the SWAT dudes to be bleeding, what was happening to the deputies on the street? And even worse, what kind of threat was presented to the citizens where these SWAT dudes were bleeding all over the place?

Point taken…some of those awesome phrases taken from Sun Tzu in *The Art of War* are better off saved for discussion around other SWAT dudes, who understand war concepts and the training and preparation involved, much as those soldiers riding in the backs of the troop transport trucks as they lumbered through the solemn empty streets of Fort Polk, slowly making their way to the wide open spaces of the airfield, where they would climb out of their growling transport vehicles and enjoy the last brief air of quiet freedom, lightly blowing across the vast runways while they slung their packs upon their backs.

Then with vivid snapshots of the past six months of training and the wife or girlfriend and family they left back home, each soldier would say their own personal goodbye to the US soil, upon which they had spent the first part of their lives, file slowly up the ramp to board their huge green winged bird that was destined to carry them far away to another land. These are the men who truly understood the deeper meaning of such a statement as "the more we sweat in time of peace, the less we bleed in time of war," especially when these men had sweated much in their training experience in this blistering hot spit of sand in the middle of Louisiana in hopes that neither they nor any of their brothers would die when they arrived in Vietnam in just a few short days.

CHAPTER 2
THE RIFLE CLUB

You will show me the path of life; in Your presence is fullness
of joy; At Your right hand are pleasures forevermore.
—Psalm 16:11

My brothers and I adjusted to the military life, which we soon learned
had affected hundreds of other families too. They lived all around us,
attended the same schools as us, and their dads drove to the army
base for work every day too. They were all intimately engaged in
the same singular purpose of preparing the many young men (just
slightly older than my older brother and I) for their commitment in
the most controversial and violent event covered in news reports each
and every day—the war in Vietnam.

While my older brother, John, and I fully understood the
potential for every soldier to die in this violent war, at the time, I did
not realize how many had just signed up for this war out of a sense of
moral obligation to fight for our country, our US Constitution, our
liberties, and our beloved flag! Now that concept just may have been
surely too much for my then eleven-year-old mind to take in.

John and I did know each soldier went to war with a Colt M16
rifle assigned to each soldier to have and to hold, to shoot and to
clean, to carry at all times in sickness and in health, in good times
and in bad, and to kill the nasty communist Vietnamese who were
trying to shove their governmental philosophies down our throats.
But we were having none of it, and to be ready if our time ever came
to join in that huge Vietnam War, we got a unique opportunity when

I was just hitting the tender age of eleven. John was merely fourteen and had only fired your basic BB guns and pellet guns up to that point.

So I have to admit, shooting a "real" gun, a gun that could really hurt and even kill someone, was a huge step for me. My fear factor was at its max when I just began to consider this opportunity, but then when I realized I may not have another chance to take a class like this, I was excited. And besides, John was going to be learning these skills too, so I figured this might be fun.

The on-base rifle club was made up of a couple dozen kids who decided they might be interested in learning how to shoot these guns that were regularly issued to our soldiers. The teachers were supposed to be pretty good at what they did, and I soon realized why. These were the rifle instructors who were entrusted to train our soldiers to go overseas to the tropical jungle and shoot all kinds of combat enemies, protect their buddies, and kill the bad men.

We sat through all the safety classes, passed the tests, and then started to learn how to work the basic bolt action .22 long rifle. To say the procedures were standardized for everyone would be a huge understatement. The firearm and equipment was inspected when we received it and carried it to the firing line. The range safety officer supervised us like a hawk with earplugs and a whistle around his neck. There was no way anybody would get off a stray shot outside of the range instructor's protocol without being beaten senseless and forever banned from any shooting range within twenty miles of the base.

No, sir, we were regimented right into the step-by-step process of load and fire when ready. "Hold your fire" meant you stopped everything and waited for the range master to tell you what to do next, nothing more and nothing less.

It was this training that helped me to understand how much later in life Forrest Gump was such a great renowned soldier as depicted in his army training. He followed each and every order exactly as given, then stopped and waited for the next order with an acknowledgment of "Yes, drill sergeant!"

For an eleven- and a fourteen-year-old, this was a perfect introduction to firearms and the shooting sports. Seemingly any chance of a misfire or dreaded accidental discharge was negated by the sheer will of every safety officer in the range building. Such negligent acts just did not happen in their presence. Mainly because these were official army firearms instructors conducting this training, and secondly because this training was attended by many children and youths of ranking officers of our base. John and I were sons of a captain, but there were children of much higher ranks as well.

And while the standard allotment of ammunition each week for each shooter was fifty rounds, it didn't take me long to realize that when the daughter of the Fort Polk commanding general was shooting with us, that standard was lifted for her and her alone. It didn't matter if those extra rounds were needed for some other worldly purpose, the general's daughter fired as many boxes of fifty rounds as she wished until she was tired of shooting. No one said anything to the contrary, unless they wished to have a personal chat with the general.

Point taken…rank has its inherent privileges!

Well, through this intense regimented training, John and I learned the basic fundamentals of marksmanship, firearms safety, and with the proper training, practice, and experience, we could achieve the basic shooting standards for pro-marksman, marksman, marksman first class, and sharpshooter. With enough time to work on the skills, we could go even further, but our time in the military was not that long. So in due time, we were working up the ranks of the ten bars of sharpshooter ranking, each of which corresponded to a different shooting position. All of this was accomplished by merely sitting through a classroom training, gearing up with a rifle and requisite fifty rounds of .22 long rifle ammo, taking our target to a shooting lane, and ever so cautiously firing one round at a time on our single target, until we had cut ten neat little holes in each of the five bull's-eye circles on our target sheet.

After we turned in the target at the conclusion of each shooting session, the instructors would score them, and we were promptly notified if we were advanced to the next level of marksmanship or not. I should really note here how only scoring hits on the targets were counted toward the minimum standard which indicated advancement to the next higher level of marksmanship. No participation trophies were handed out to any shooters for just showing up on any given Saturday morning.

And we were constantly reminded a .22 long rifle bullet could fly a mile if you were to shoot it up into the air and subsequently kill a man when it returned to earth. All in all, the important takeaway from this experience for both John and me was about how we could put in the time and effort to learn a difficult skill, and with even more hard work and effort, we could develop those skills into something that we might use to some benefit later in life.

For John, he later became an accomplished soldier, certified in advanced combat training at Fort Hood, Texas, airborne training at Fort Bragg, North Carolina, and finally a candidate for Army Ranger Training (one of the special forces divisions of the US Army).

For me, I later used these same learned skills after earning a position on the SWAT team to try out for the sniper unit, for which I am deeply grateful to have had the opportunity. Reflecting back on this period of time and seeing the incredible difference this training and practice made in my life, I have often pondered if the men who showed up every Saturday morning at the Fort Polk Rifle Club had any idea how much they would influence the lives and direction of the youths who they were mentoring. Better yet, I have often thought about the joy on their faces if they had been present when I was putting into practice the lessons learned to qualify for the sheriff's office sniper unit. I am sure they would have been proud! But I got ahead of myself. I will go into that later.

Point taken…if we put in the hours of hard work and training, we will gain the privilege of learning skills which may keep us alive in combat. Not bad for an eleven- and fourteen-year-old to understand and truly appreciate.

Second point taken, if we just showed up, participation trophies were not provided.

CHAPTER 3

WHAT DO I WANT TO BE WHEN I GROW UP?

I am the true vine, and My Father is the vinedresser. Every branch in me that does not bear fruit He takes away, and every branch that bears fruit He prunes, that it may bear more fruit. You are already clean because of the word which I have spoken to you. Abide in Me, and I in you. As the branch cannot bear fruit of itself, unless it abides in the vine, neither can you, unless you abide in Me.

—John 15:1–4

Fast-forward to a few years later when I attended a west central Florida high school, home of the Fighting Buccaneers. During my final two years of high school, I began to get serious about figuring out what direction I should go in the years afterward. I completely understand how so many youths can get wrapped up in confusion during this period in their lives because that is where I remained for most of the time.

Not surprisingly, I even spent some quality time speaking with a local Army recruiter to explore those options, which looked very interesting and exciting for a minute. However, I was talked out of that direction and strongly encouraged to look at college options without any concern for the expense of college, even though I had believed the option of college paid for by the US Army seemed like an optimal choice. But when I looked at college, I still didn't know which courses to take for my career choice, not to mention that my high school course selection did not support the level of academics needed for a college student. I had no confidence in my ability to perform at the college level.

Suffice it to say, I looked at many different options which didn't seem too difficult and required minimal education. That was good enough to get me started. Why not keep my aspirations low, and they'll inevitably become much easier to reach? Right?

I eventually came across several friends in my high school who were actively participating in a local police cadet program (explorer program) starting at the local sheriff's office for young men and women who wished to learn more about law enforcement as a possible career choice. This caught my attention, and ultimately I enrolled in and completed a basic explorer training academy and spent two and a half years with the explorer program while finishing high school and attending my first two years of college at a local community college.

Ultimately, since I completed community college with an AS in criminal justice and an AA, my college confidence was boosted tremendously. So I attended two more years of college to complete a four-year criminology program at Florida State University, a college internship which lasted a full six months at the Tallahassee State Attorney's Office and thirteen weeks of police basic recruit training before I was ready to apply for employment as an entry-level police officer. Now I was ready to step in the door at any law enforcement agency in the state, so after being turned down by just about every state agency due to equal employment opportunity quotas, I applied to the Pasco Sheriff's Office to get hired on as an entry-level deputy sheriff.

Most of those stories of my early career, I may share in a different format, but soon after my hiring (at slightly more than minimum wage), I discovered our police agency had a riot control squad for civil disturbance problems, inevitably related to the protests of angry citizens during the Vietnam War during the 1970s. I knew this from a photograph taken of a group of senior officers holding full-face shield helmets, full-size riot batons, and clear riot shields (in a grainy black-and-white photo), which hung in a dusty black frame on the wall of the administration hallway. This was the hallway where people had their names added to special plaques, and photos were hung to commemorate special events which happened during each sheriff's term in office.

After the riot squad had not been called out for any huge riots or protests in a long while, such as what happened in Kent State or Berkeley or elsewhere, and after the riot equipment had been long ago retired to the dusty closet of a patrol room for several years, the sheriff decided to change the purpose of the riot squad, and the riot squad became a SWAT team. This was in 1979 when much of law enforcement was striving to gain recognition as a "profession" with minimum standards for education, training, and ultimately better pay scales. Our agency, the Pasco County Sheriff's Office, was not a large agency and struggled for the higher levels of recognition and professionalism which were granted to many of the surrounding counties, such as Pinellas County (Clearwater and St. Petersburg) and Hillsborough County (Tampa).

Many of the senior deputies, detectives, and even some sergeants who had gained a position on the riot squad eventually decided they may not appreciate the work hours or the increased workload of a more active SWAT team, which was subject to being called out for high-risk incidents at all hours of the day or night. And so a slow transition began over time to gradually replace some of the older men on the team with a little more "younger" blood. This transition involved more than a change of personnel; it also involved a change in the culture of the team as many other agencies developed SWAT teams of their own and actively pursued the supplemental training and equipment which prepared these new younger members of a specialty team to successfully perform their special operations assignments with optimal success.

CHAPTER 4
THE ROOKIE DEPUTY

You whom I have taken from the ends of the earth, And called from
its farthest regions, And said to you, you are My servant, I have
chosen you and have not cast you away: Fear not, for I am with
you; Be not dismayed for I am your God, I will strengthen you, Yes,
I will help you, I will uphold you with My righteous right hand.
—Isaiah 41:9–10

Since I had taken my big first step into law enforcement on April 2,
1983, when the sheriff of Pasco County hired me, the timing was
right for me to step into a position to replace one of the older guys on
the riot squad who no longer wished to volunteer for such a position.
However, there were a few experiences which transpired in the mean-
time before that opportunity was put before me. The timing was
especially critical because I was not eligible to even join the SWAT
team until I had acquired two years of law enforcement experience,
and I had been a member of the sheriff's office for one year. This
standard was developed by many SWAT teams and was utilized to
serve two main purposes.

The first purpose: to serve two years in the law enforcement
profession, allowed the "rookie" officer to serve long enough so he
or she could experience plenty of those high-risk adrenaline-charged
situations where high-speed critical decisions must be made in an
instant and where the adrenaline surges through your body for hours
after the event. The exposure to such situations truly demonstrate
whether the deputy can survive through the critical thinking and

the aftermath without any significant trauma. In most cases, the survival through such incidents is a reflection on the level of training provided to the deputy and the mentality of the deputy as well. For those members who emerge from such a critical incident in a mental daze, emotional wreck, and spiritual disaster, the choice for their future is rather plain, and they are not made out to be SWAT officers. But for those officers who finish a high-risk, life-threatening confrontation with a zest for more of the same and a *whoop-whoop*-war scream, high-fiving their partners to celebrate their survival of that mess where they could have just died, well, those are the ones who tend to make the best SWAT dudes…

Now, the one-year requirement with the agency was implemented because once the officer has experienced two years in the business and encountered the life-threatening situations along the way, he or she may decide to change to a different agency for whatever reason. Once beginning service at a new agency, the newbie officer is observed by existing team members during their first year to gauge their tactical knowledge and sense in the routine course of their work. Thus, before being considered for membership on the team, the team members must offer their personal observations of whether the applicant may be a positive contributor to the team, or whether the applicant is a tactical disaster looking for a place to happen. In such instances, where you must depend on each other with your lives in each and every callout or search warrant, nobody on the team would want to be paired on a perimeter with a tactical disaster or go through a doorway with someone who couldn't get out of their own way, let alone cover your six (back side), hence, the reason for the one-year observation period with the agency.

So as a rookie deputy once hired, I was put through a training program which entailed riding with a senior deputy to gain more exposure to the policies and procedures, paperwork, and the culture of our agency, until I was deemed ready to be "cut loose" on my own. In our agency, during the 1980s, they trained you with a sink-or-swim mentality. Either you caught on to the job and were placed in a solo deputy assignment, or you didn't, in which case, you were released and told to practice for your next job by rehearsing the simple lines, "paper or plastic?"

That was a running joke among the training officers during my time of orientation, which many didn't find very funny until and if they eventually succeeded to advance out of the program.

The more experienced designated trainer on my squad was Scott, who had spent time in several detective positions and, at the time of our training, also held a sniper position on the SWAT team. This was all just too convenient as I had unlimited time to ask Scott questions about the team, how he gained a position on the team, was there a height requirement, what exciting callouts did they get to go on, how often did they get a call out, and did they get to carry and shoot cool guns and stuff.

Although I am absolutely sure he was tired of my run-on questions after the first day, he tolerated me mainly because he had no other choice. I was his "turtle" for the duration…until he passed me or failed me. My future hung on his opinion of whether he believed I would succeed as a deputy.

Down the road, Scott did have the opportunity to pass me around to some of the other senior members of our squad to soak up as much knowledge and experience as I could before I was finally ready to spread my wings and fly on my own. The details of the whole training experience will have to wait for another time, but suffice it to say, they were full of crazy happenings and fun times. But the day of my release finally came about four weeks after I had started when I walked into the patrol room one morning, sat through roll call, fully expecting to ride along for another shift with one of the senior guys on our squad, until Sergeant Sides asked me if I had a shotgun.

I told him, "No, sir!"

So he responded in his thick southern drawl, "Then I'd recommend you sign one out for today 'cause you're ridin' solo today, son."

With that, he tossed me the keys to car number 80, an older green-and-white Ford LTD parked out in our parking lot with a single big blue light on the rooftop, looking like a bubblegum machine from the old days. As I carried my file box of paperwork out to my "new" mobile office, shotgun in hand, I closely looked at the former rental car which now sported a drab green-and-white paint job, with green lettering of "SHERIFF" and bold green striping down the sides of the fenders. The chipped and flaking lettering reflected the years of use this vehicle had seen as a spare vehicle during its prior lifetime of service. Yet this former rental vehicle now had a new lease on life while it still had that uncharacteristic, tacky bright-red velvet interior that seemed more suited to offering a comfy place to sit for a nice older retired couple for their excursions around town, shopping, church, bingo, etc. No, this car definitely didn't look like the first assigned patrol vehicle for a young twenty-two-year-old newly-hired deputy starting out in his first law enforcement job.

But the good news was…I had successfully passed my training process, and that was very good! But the bad news unfortunately became very apparent, very soon. I had received only a smidgen of the knowledge and wisdom, which I would ultimately require to really succeed at this career. Keep in mind, neither the police academy in Tallahassee nor the sheriff's office training process provided me with any more common sense which I had when I graduated from Florida State University. And while I had met many experienced officers during my training and orientation, I learned from these meetings that higher education was not always so helpful in many of the roles which I would step into during my future assignments, including SWAT assignments.

From this point onward, I had to gain my wisdom from the voice of experience, the Holy Spirit and the school of hard knocks. You get the idea!

As I moved onward, I soon had the opportunity to respond to a high-risk situation involving a domestic violence call which had escalated very quickly into a violent confrontation inside a home in the Orchid Lake community. During the violence, the wife had escaped from the home and left the husband inside the house, barricaded, with guns in the house as well. The deputies on the scene called the sergeant, and after he arrived, he soon decided to call for the SWAT team to set a perimeter while negotiators tried to "talk him out."

Since I was the "rookie" on the scene, I was relegated to the outer perimeter of the operation where all I could see was whoever left the scene or whoever arrived on the scene. I was a glorified armed access control security guard for the evening. Well, soon enough, different types of patrol cars began to arrive as they pulled alongside me and asked where they could safely park before getting geared up to move into whatever assignment was in store for them. As I greeted the arriving deputies and detectives, I immediately generated a conclusion which made a lasting impression upon me. As each highly respected deputy, detective, and specialty unit deputy pulled up, not a single team member talked "down" to me, but each one presented themselves as humble, kind, or a joking attitude. Yes, each one of these well-respected officers was far, far superior to me in education, experience, and exposure to high-risk situations, yet they spoke to me as a partner and equal.

Here, our squad had responded to a simple domestic dispute gone bad, with a bad guy barricaded inside the house, and these guys were coming out to save the day and face a potential shooting situation to take our guy into custody. Yet they each had the most casual, cool-as-a-cucumber attitude as they went about the business of taking over the scene. I was somewhat surprised, but as I met the various arrivals, another idea crossed my mind. Each SWAT dude also had a reputation within our agency for being knowledgeable, proficient, and very competent as a law enforcement officer. Many of them even knew who I was, which seemed surprising to me, but made sense considering our agency had just under a hundred sworn deputies and detectives (sworn law enforcement personnel).

I figured out very soon that these guys (they all happened to be men) were the cream of the crop of our law enforcement family. They were the best we had to offer, especially when it came to backing up our patrol forces on the streets. These guys were there on our SWAT team for a reason and not just randomly picked as needed to fill a vacancy on the team.

Suddenly, I had a goal!

If, indeed, I was to stay here at the Pasco Sheriff's Office, I needed a goal to set my sights on to aspire to…I needed to get onto this team, come hell or high water, and hopefully not both at the same time. I wanted to be the one who my peers looked to when the public called 911, and then when my colleagues responded, if the situation was too hot to handle, they would call me and the team to help resolve the crisis of the moment.

For me, this was a watershed moment, a revelation, and an awakening. I had a goal!

CHAPTER 5
STRIVING FOR THE GOAL

Therefore submit yourselves to every ordinance of man
for the Lord's sake, whether to the king as supreme, or to
governors, as to those who are sent by him for the punishment
of evildoers and for the praise of those who do good. For
this is the will of God, that by doing good you may put to
silence the ignorance of foolish men as free, yet not using
liberty as a cloak for vice, but as bondservants of God.
—1 Peter 2:13–16

Although I didn't realize it at the time, I was working to develop my SWAT mentality from that point forward. I began reading books on the topic, reading books on tactical operations, books on high-risk incidents, the psychology of hostage takers, etc. I was rereading my college books as well, which after seeking to major in criminology, I had minored in psychology and sociology, which provided much background in behavioral analysis for the study of deviant behavior and those behavior patterns which I was dealing with on an almost daily basis. I became like a sponge, soaking up any information about our team's members and talking with them at each chance I had. I wanted to learn all I could from them.

As my schooling progressed, I took a hard look at my firearms knowledge and personal fitness. While I had been basically physically inactive in high school, except for the absolute effort which was required to obtain a passing grade in physical education, I took some advice and personal coaching from my older brother when I began attending the local community college. I began lifting weights at a local health club and running. During the course of my time in Pasco Hernando Community College (now a state college), I ran several 5K events, even a ten-mile race, and a couple 10Ks. Fortunately, through my two years at Florida State, I continued to run and played intramural soccer as well. During my first year in law enforcement, I continued running just out of habit, and I hadn't settled into the deadly sedentary routine which grips so many cops early in their careers.

Through the frequent conversations with the younger more active members of the SWAT team, I realized they all took personal responsibility for their own personal fitness by training on their own, during their "off duty" time. As a tight-knit group, they did it not only for their personal benefit but as an obligation to their fellow team members. Just like a military squad, they took care of each other by keeping themselves in the best possible condition, so they were physically capable of rendering whatever help was needed to any of their buddies whenever help was needed. This dedication was something which I had noticed, which was not so prevalent among the squads of deputies on the streets or just not common. Those close squads on the street were few and far between, and I realized how much I wished to be part of such an elite group who took pride in their fitness, marksmanship abilities, and tactical experience. Yes, I was just hit with another watershed moment…thank you, God!

So in addition to picking up the pace of my fitness training and seeking tactical knowledge, I began spending more time taking my Smith & Wesson six shooter revolver out to the shooting range. To give you a little background on this topic as I had mentioned previously, my extensive rifle training at the age of eleven was the only firearms training I had ever received, except for some casual target shooting in the backyard with my older brother. So when I began training in the police academy after college at Florida State, I was a total rookie when it came to handguns.

We went through the mandatory classroom safety training at the police academy, 'til we finally ventured out onto the open sandy shooting range under the hot Tallahassee sun, firing round after round of practice ammunition at paper targets from the various distances over and over again. Perhaps one reason I did not seem to take this training so seriously was the fact we shot from various close distances but then stepped back to take aim from the twenty-five- and fifty-yard lines. To this date, I have no idea why they ever thought I should be firing a gun fifty yards at *any* bad guys, terrorists, or hostage takers. Despite the best efforts of our expert firearms trainer, Palmer Newton, I emerged at the end of the firearms training sessions with a passing score in the mid-eighties, thanks to some wild shots that went over the target stands, no doubt from the prone position at the fifty-yard line. The trainers suggested to avoid pulling my trigger unless I was "really sure" of where that bullet was going. This sounded so much like the US army firearms training staff. I expected one of them to tell me that an errant shot fired into the air could potentially land a mile away and kill a man!

Now realizing that I was tasked with enforcing laws in my rural Pasco County, I decided that maybe some practice with my issued six shooter was needed before I ended up in some OK Corral scenario. After all, I didn't want to be the one known for shooting anything and everything *but* the bad guy or the horse he rode in on.

Truth be told, I hadn't done much shooting when in college because I did not own nor could I afford a gun. Since I started my career at a pay rate close to minimum wage and below poverty level at the total of $13,500 per year, there wasn't much chance this cowboy would be acquiring a gun of his own for several years. Thankfully I had enough cash for buying my own ammunition, and during these early years, I entered shooting competitions with my duty gun, my .38 Special revolver with a four-inch barrel. No need to worry about those "unlimited revolver" or "automatic pistol" shooting categories, as those were way out of my budget range.

As the months passed, I was very fortunate to solicit some quality coaching from a good friend and sniper on the SWAT team as he had extensive experience with handguns, and he understood my end goals. I will always be appreciative and thankful for the coaching and guidance of my friend, Kurt. While I learned how to improve my scores with my revolver, he pointed me toward some of the shooting competitions offered in our part of the state. Within a short time, I entered some of these competitions to further hone my skills and fundamentals. My handgun shooting skills came up to a more respectable level, one which seemed much more commensurate with a SWAT dude.

Just a few years later, while shooting in a competitive league, I was fortunate to shoot with a good friend who always wanted to be a sniper on the team, who was well known as an outstanding hand-gunner in his own right. His coaching was instrumental in lifting my abilities, confidence, and shooting scores much higher than I believed possible. He was recognized among the "Governor's Twenty," top twenty law enforcement shooters in the State of Florida. Joe was an excellent shooter, a good friend, and later in my career, he was my patrol captain too.

The more I hung around some of these team members, I found myself getting invited to their workouts as they prepped for their annual physical qualification testing. Sometimes we met at different school sites to make use of their running tracks or use the monkey bars on the playgrounds. We would often put on the "flak vest," which was standard issue to the team members, and run around the track as many laps as we could handle before collapsing in the heat. Then we got really crazy and ran laps with the flak vest *and* a gas mask. As you might expect, the gas mask forced us to suck in all our oxygen through a filter, which was much easier said than done. This was especially true when you try to do a rapid air exchange while running…it was nearly impossible to keep an adequate supply of oxygen to fuel your red blood cells for more than a couple laps around the track. If I'm not mistaken, this would be how the fitness scientists learned about anerobic fitness at the famed Cooper Cardiovascular Clinics in Dallas, Texas. From their research, they discovered the changes which happen when you push your body despite the lack of oxygen to fuel your muscles as you run.

That feeling of wearing a thirty-pound vest with ceramic plates in the front and rear, wrapped tightly around my upper body, with a rubber mask strapped just as tightly on my head, trying to move my body forward around the track, with that eerie sound of my foot tapping the ground in rhythmic cadence while I literally sucked each breath of air through the filters of my mask was an experience beyond claustrophobic. It was challenging, even for a young twenty-three-year-old, weighing only 150 pounds, with all the drive and determination to prove he had the "right stuff" to make it on this elite team. Perhaps the right motivator was just knowing that if I made it on the team, these very heroes working out with me would be my teammates working alongside me on each future callout of the SWAT team. Yes, that was all the real motivation I needed, and it proved to be effective enough for me as the future unfolded.

CHAPTER 6
QUALIFICATION TIME

You did not choose Me, but I chose you and appointed you that
you should go and bear fruit, and that your fruit should remain,
that whatever you ask the Father in My name He may give you.
These things I command you, that you love one another.
—John 15:16–17

As mentioned in the rookie deputy training process, the training
was mostly verbal, rarely written (other than the standard reports
completed on patrol), and in the end, I passed or failed. Well, the
SWAT team had "unwritten" rules for qualification that were later
documented completely for the benefit of all those who wished to
try out for the team in subsequent years. Those rules still stand today
as follows:

1. Each applicant wishing to pass qualification standards to be considered for a position on the SWAT team must have a minimum of two years of law enforcement experience (military experience may be considered) and a minimum of one-year employment with the Pasco Sheriff's Office in a sworn law enforcement position.

2. Each applicant must submit to tests of physical fitness, firearms marksmanship, psychological assessment, and oral board review, which must be successfully passed. While the fitness test, the psychological test,

and the oral board are all pass/fail tests, the firearms test must be passed by a score of 90 percent or better. (Hence, my need for the extra work to bring up my shooting scores prior to the qualification process.)

While the qualifications were physically challenging, I couldn't help but feel the competitive tension in the air as I ran around the track at the local high school. At this point, I only remember four of us competing during the run, which was a standard mile and a half. In some ways, running six laps on a track is extremely difficult from just the boredom factor alone. Secondly, the risk of losing count of your laps is an issue too. Was that lap 3 or 4 that I just finished? That is just way too much pressure.

The other part of this physical fitness test just involved lots of sit-ups and pushups mainly because our agency could not afford the raw materials for an obstacle course or the heavy equipment to construct such a course. So we just got down on the track, and while one candidate held our ankles to the ground, we wildly flew upward to touch our elbows to our knees, then flung ourselves back 'til our lower backs touched the asphalt track again in rapid succession for a full minute.

After all the testing, I returned to the office to meet with Lieutenant Weinberg for the last phase of the test day: the oral board. Now my stress about this part of the test was all based on the fact I had not finished my second year of experience with the sheriff's office. So I was hoping he would give me consideration for a position on the team just based on how dedicated I had been to attend several SWAT training days during the past year and then for my efforts to meet with the team members during the past several months to partner with them during their fitness training while they prepared for their annual SWAT team requalification testing, or maybe he would at least give me some consideration for a position on a waiting list for future selection if a position was to open later in the year.

Words can't describe how excited and surprised I was when Lieutenant Weinberg welcomed me to the team, subject to the sheriff's approval. He told me they were filling two slots on the team, and my friend, Bobby Spanos, would be taking the other slot. I was elated and left that testing day, thanking my Heavenly Father for His grace and mercy to give me the drive to try out for the team that day. I couldn't believe it, and I couldn't wait to begin training with my new team.

On April 22, 1985, just twenty days after my two-year anniversary with the agency, I was officially appointed to the team by our chief deputy, Jim Francis, via a very brief memo. The memo advised me to arrange to obtain my required equipment from Lieutenant Weinberg, so I followed up with excitement the next time I saw the lieutenant in the patrol room. I proudly asked him when I could pick up my SWAT equipment from him, hoping some of the guys in the patrol room could hear me and realized I had made it onto the SWAT team.

Lieutenant Weinberg responded, "What equipment are you talking about?"

I was suddenly confused.

"Special weapons?" I asked.

He asked me back, "You have your service revolver?"

"Yes, sir!" I knew that answer quickly and confidently.

He continued, "You have a shotgun, right?"

Instantly I was so glad after my first year with the agency; I joined in with two friends on my squad to buy our own personal shotguns from a holiday sale at an Oshman's Sporting Goods store in Clearwater. We each bought a brand-new Winchester Defender twelve-gauge shotgun for only $168.00…a price that would be impossible to come by in today's market.

I responded with detail, "Yes, sir! A Winchester Defender 12 gauge!"

Lieutenant retorted, "There you go! You have everything you need."

I slowly walked away before I embarrassed myself any further in front of my SWAT team commander and anybody else within earshot. That whole conversation just left me with so many unanswered questions. Why did the chief deputy (sheriff's executive assistant) tell me in the memo to get my equipment and SWAT gear from

Lieutenant Weinberg? If I was replacing somebody on the team, what happened to their old equipment? Didn't they turn it in? Was the lieutenant really just going to surprise me and Bobby and buy us new camo BDUs and gear?

Okay, I needed to stop the dreaming and come back to reality. These wild ideas were getting me nowhere.

Ultimately, I eventually showed up at my first official SWAT team training day as an official member of the team. Bobby and I talked to the team members, getting to know them, and finally got some straight answers to all or most of our questions. The other team members went digging through their SWAT gear bags, stashed deep in the trunks of their patrol cars, and pulled out various sundry parts and pieces, which if all totaled may have outfitted one-fifth of a SWAT dude with the bare essentials. By the time I collected the spare parts and pieces, I had the following items for my SWAT gear:

- One woodland camo shirt, size XXL (three sizes too big)
- One nylon Velcro closure belt, size small (one size too small)
- One double speed strip ammo holder with Velcro closure
- Two Velcro belt keepers (to wrap around the inner pants belt and the outer gun belt to keep them together)
- Thirteen spare rounds of .38 special ammunition
- One box of five rounds, 12-gauge rifled slugs for shotgun ammunition. These do a lot of damage on impact.
- Two boxes of five rounds each, 12-gauge 00 buck shotgun ammunition
- One OD green plastic canteen (no holder, just a canteen. No idea what liquids had been in this canteen or what may be required to disinfect it prior to my use)

- One wire gun cleaning brush attachment for nine-millimeter caliber (lucky for me, it could also fit a .38 caliber.)
- One mostly empty plastic bottle of Hoppe's gun cleaner solvent with enough for maybe three cleanings, if I was lucky.

So with my newly acquired SWAT gear and, even better, my answers to so many pressing SWAT questions, I was ready to begin my journey with this new band of brothers (later to include a SWAT sister, as well). Little did I know this partnership would become a vital part of my career and my life for the next twenty-six years.

Silhouette view of Deputy Jeff Tanner initiating rapid entry into the dark interior of the Clearwater Fire Department Training Tower while beginning tactical stair ascent training. Bulky equipment bag at waist level is the gas mask carrier. The .38 cal duty revolver pointed straight up is NOT proper form for a tactical entry per current tactics. The baseball cap was standard headgear for all callouts as the agency could not afford ballistic helmets for many of the early years of our team. SWAT training, 1986.

CHAPTER 7

MY FIRST BARRICADED SUBJECT SWAT CALLOUT

The law of the Lord is perfect, converting the soul; The
testimony of the Lord is sure, making wise the simple;
The statutes of the Lord are right, rejoicing the heart;
The commandment of the Lord is pure, enlightening the
eyes; The fear of the Lord is clean, enduring forever; The
judgments of the Lord are true and righteous altogether.
—Psalm 19:7–9

Although most SWAT callouts at this time involved barricaded subjects, which don't occur very often, most of our SWAT activity at this
time involved training days. And we had the fortunate opportunity
to train together one full workday each month. But we had an exciting barricade situation on January 1, 1986, where a twenty-eight-
year-old Zephyrhills man had been arrested early on January 1 for
trespassing after he confronted his estranged wife in a local restaurant
and then refused to leave. So after he had been released on bond from
the local jail, he went to his wife's home to await her return.

Well, when the wife went to her home to get some clothes for
her children, she saw the husband's truck parked nearby, and the
curtains moved inside her living room. Fortunately, nobody had
stepped inside the home yet, and the deputy who had escorted her
to her home set a perimeter and notified his supervisor. Ultimately
the supervisor could not coax the husband out of the house, so rather
than risk his life going in after the husband, he called the SWAT team.

This callout was interesting to me because it dragged on for three and a half hours into the night while the patrol lieutenant barked on the bullhorn to attempt his negotiations with the stubborn husband.

And I thought bullhorns were only used for dramatic effect on TV, but here I had the fine opportunity to experience firsthand as a respected supervisor was frustrated beyond belief while he ordered and begged the man to come out of his home so we could all go home. Needless to say, the lieutenant was not so patient with this guy, but the wife had believed her husband may be barricaded inside with a rifle, which made things more interesting. We always took life very seriously when they talked about the bad guy being armed with a rifle...just something about a firearm that can fire a bullet for a mile and still come down and kill a man made us pay closer attention to any potential threats with his rifle.

We had the opportunity in this callout to listen to the negotiation tactics very, very loudly and clearly as the lieutenant yelled at the suspect to come out so we could all go home, but in this case, they worked, and eventually the husband came out, and we were all able to go home. I don't believe his surrender had anything to do with his consideration in ruining all of our team members' plans for the New Year's Day holiday, but at that point, we were just happy to go home and sleep.

This was just one case where I really wished the suspect would follow through on his divorce so we would not have to respond to any more of his domestic violence calls. This case was just too dangerous for his wife, especially with the lengthy history between the two.

The unusual element in this callout involved the negotiations conducted over a bullhorn so all could hear. Most negotiations involved placement of a tactical "throw phone," two-way radio system into the environment of the barricaded subject, so the negotiators can speak directly with the subject. In this way, all the negotiations can be recorded over the two-way radio system, and if the subject should hang up the "phone," the negotiators can still listen in via the hidden speaker in the phone. So if the subject is discussing any sort of escape plan or other aggressive tactics, the negotiators would hear and relay that information to the tactical commander.

As I listened to the negotiations, I quickly learned there was not a lot of special technique involved but usually a high degree of patience and pestering the subject to push them to surrender without violence. It isn't rocket science, and although the dialogue has to be geared to the appropriate situation, usually the negotiator has ample opportunity to insert his or her own style into the conversation. A strong background in psychology is helpful for breaking through some of the more difficult subjects who seem very resistant to giving up, which makes this area of law enforcement very intriguing. Hence, with my background, I always "enjoyed" the opportunities to listen in on negotiations whenever possible to attempt to figure out the inner workings of the barricaded subject or hostage taker. For my involvement in these operations, this was just another reason why I enjoyed resolving these types of high-risk situations.

Dep. Jeff Tanner, on scene preparing for sniper deployment with my Remington .308 cal sniper rifle, at a SWAT callout in Hudson, FL. Note the light gray backpack loaded with sandbags, binoculars, and extra ammunition, was previously used a few years prior to carry books and school materials at F.S.U. Another example of using recycled materials for SWAT duty gear due to lack of a SWAT budget. SWAT callout, 1986.

PT TIMES ■ THURSDAY, JANUARY 2, 1986   **3**

Man arrested near Zephyrhills after stand-off with deputies

By STEPHEN HEGARTY
St. Petersburg Times Staff Writer

ZEPHYRHILLS — A Dade City man was arrested Wednesday after a 3½-hour stand-off with sheriff's deputies. The man is accused of threatening his estranged wife, breaking into her home and refusing to leave, a Pasco sheriff's spokesman said.

Karl Comer Keith, 28, of 192 Terry Road, finally surrendered to deputies and left his wife's home near Zephyrhills at about 12:40 p.m. Wednesday, said spokesman Robert Loeffler. Although Keith was not armed, the

> **Karl Keith already had been arrested in Zephyrhills on Wednesday morning and charged with trespassing after harassing his estranged wife in a Zephyrhills restaurant, a sheriff's spokesman said.**

sheriff's SWAT team was called in because Keith's wife had indicated that her husband might be armed and dangerous, Loeffler said.

KEITH WAS charged with burglary and was taken to the East Pasco Detention Center, where he was held without bail.

Keith had been arrested in Zephyrhills on Wednesday morning and charged with trespassing after harassing his estranged wife in a Zephyrhills restaurant, Loeffler said. The Dade City man was released on the trespassing charge early Wednesday after posting $250 bail.

Keith and his wife, Mona Sue Keith, are getting a divorce, Loeffler said.

AFTER HE was released from jail early Wednesday, Keith apparently went looking for his wife, Loeffler said. Keith telephoned his mother's house in Dade City, where his wife was staying with the couple's two children, ages 2 years and 5 months. Keith threatened his wife on the telephone, Loeffler said.

Mrs. Keith called the sheriff's department Wednesday and requested an escort so she could go to her house on Cass Road just north of Zephyrhills to get some clothes for the children, Loeffler said. When Mrs. Keith and the deputy arrived at her house, Mrs. Keith thought her husband was in the house because she noticed his truck nearby and noticed that the curtains in her home had been moved.

LOEFFLER SAID Keith was inside the house and refused to come out for nearly 3½ hours. Finally, after speaking to Keith with a bullhorn, sheriff's Lt. Tom Bissett was able to coax Keith out of the house, Loeffler said.

Loeffler said that in recent months, sheriff's deputies have responded several times to complaints involving Keith and his estranged wife.

Loeffler said Keith had been on probation from a resisting-arrest charge in Orlando.

45

CHAPTER 8

THE MAJOR SEARCH WARRANT IN BLANTON

Here is My servant, whom I uphold, My chosen one in whom
I delight; I will put My Spirit on him, and He will bring justice
to the nations. He will not shout or cry out, or raise his voice in
the streets. A bruised reed He will not break, and a smoldering
wick He will not snuff out. In faithfulness He will bring forth
justice, He will not falter or be discouraged till He establishes
justice on earth. In His teaching the islands will put their hope.
—Isaiah 42:1–4 (NIV)

Soon thereafter, I had the opportunity—about a month after the
last barricaded subject callout—to take part in a large search warrant
operation, which had been initiated by our drug investigations unit
of the sheriff's office. The investigation was focused in the rural east-
ern portion of our county, north of the county seat, Dade City. The
community was a small area where seemingly everybody knew everybody else, although it was a combination of farms, ranches, orange
and other citrus groves, and a small housing community with lots of
small homes of the two-bedroom, one-bathroom variety for starting
families. The homes were set on a close pattern of streets with no
more than ten homes set side by side in the small residential subdivi-
sion, and a cluster of six or seven parallel streets surrounded by large
pastures, grazing cattle, and orange groves.

Near this community of homes, a cocaine processing and distribution center had sprung up where they received powder cocaine

from Tampa, cut it with mannitol, inositol, or whatever suitable cuts were available and cooked this solution into crack cocaine. The crack cocaine was packaged for ready distribution to street vendors in the local Dade City, Lacoochee, and Zephyrhills communities. This was during the time of the beginning of the immense crack trade which was conducted for years on the east side of Pasco County and elsewhere throughout the state, which made many distributors very, very wealthy and left many crack users bankrupt, destitute, and eventually dead.

I took into consideration—at this time, not many SWAT teams were utilized for search warrants—as they had initially been utilized after dumping their rarely utilized riot gear as a supplemental force for the patrol forces whenever difficult situations were encountered which were beyond the skill set of the patrol units. Also during the time up 'til now, most narcotics investigation units operated under such an intense veil of secrecy and darkness; they rarely involved any other deputies or detectives in any of their operations for fear that the secret details of their operations may leak out, hence the old adage of many a vice detective during this time: loose lips sink ships.

It was a well-known fact; all you needed to do to see a vice detective go berserk was spill the secrets of their undercover operation which they had been working for months and months only to have it become "front-page news" in the blink of an eye. I'm sure you have heard of that phrase, "hell hath no fury," which you may have thought referred to a woman scorned. Well, it could just as well emerge after the wrath of a vice detective after their investigation was blown by somebody's loose lips.

Throughout most of the briefing and SWAT team preparation leading up to this "raid," the team was introduced to a Ryder rental box truck with a roll-up door in the rear, which could be opened quickly enough to allow all the team members to jump out the back tailgate and pounce on the bad guys in mere seconds...in a perfect world. Aha! It was the ancient "Trojan horse" tactic. Simple. Effective and still, at our point in time (mid-1980s), a very ancient tactic.

Now to the best of my knowledge, this idea had been suggested for our operation by someone above my pay grade, and given my pay grade, that was not very difficult to find! The premise was to deliver our team to the search warrant location without arousing much, if any, suspicion. In this way, the team could confront and secure as many people as possible using the element of surprise on the enemy before anyone could initiate any violent action against us or begin to destroy any of the drugs on the property. I guessed, in my tactically developing mind, our friend, Sun Tzu, didn't have any better ideas up his kimono sleeve that might help us deploy any quicker than the Trojan horse.

So during the practice training, we stood at the ready in the back of the truck while a designated detective riding in the cargo compartment flung the door open, and we all rushed out the back of the truck at once. It seemed both cumbersome and confusing at first, but after a few practice runs, we began to get a pattern that worked well. Since the truck intended to pull into the property facing toward the houses and trailers, which we needed to secure first, we just lined up alongside the sides of the truck, jumped to the ground, and peeled around each side in two line formations.

We SWAT dudes tend to catch on quicker to tactics when we can file along in a line. Maybe it has something to do with us being really good at follow-the-leader or "Simon says." Plus following a line gave us a good head start to the target houses before we bashed in the front doors and went running inside yelling, "Sheriff's office, search warrant!" Little did I know at this point in my SWAT career how many hundreds and hundreds of times that phrase would become our team's "calling card" over the next twenty-plus years.

After all the rehearsals, we loaded in the van, discussed the potential suspects, weapons, and dogs we were likely to confront during this mission, and we loaded up to proceed to the surveillance house in the midst of the small Blanton community which over-looked the target location, crack cocaine distribution center. All, that is, except one team member who was having some serious "second thoughts" about this mission. He had fear written all over his face and through all his body language as well to the point we could prac-tically see the yellow tint of cowardice in his skin tone. Even though at the time of my hiring, two and a half years prior, he outranked me by seventy-one slots on the deputy roster. With considerable seniority and experience above me, he was focused on the many uncontrollable variables in this raid plan. Therefore, he decided to back out of this mission rather than support his fellow team members.

I must admit, the game plan for this raid did have a lot of options, even though the detectives had been watching the operations from a "safe house" for the past two weeks, and they had spotted some pit bull protection dogs, guns, and lots of bad guys. But somehow when the Chicken Little coward backed out, the team's response was universal. We all agreed; Chicken Little was off the team. In reaching this agreement, we all seemed much more determined to stick together and hit this place together as a team and to do this as professionally as we could do it.

Point taken! When your team faces a challenging operation, and more adversity is thrown their way, a true band of brothers will come together as an integral unit and bond more closely than before! Our team knew one very important element of truth when the vice unit initially called upon us to help initiate this search warrant. This era was a time when typically the vice detectives did all the investigating to develop the probable cause for their warrants, took their cases to the State Attorney's Office and essentially wrote the search warrants (with the aid of a speed typist who took an oath of silence before she put the elements in the search warrant and affidavit). Then the detectives loaded up their raid tools, sledgehammers, battering rams, raid jackets, and everything they needed, and they went out to the target location to "hit" the target themselves. So since they had this major operation, and they called upon our team, we understood if we did a good job for them, they may just begin to consider changing their standard operating procedures to utilize our team more often for search warrants. Or at least, they may use our team more often than in the past, which was "almost never!" That became our goal as we trained and readied ourselves for this operation, which was very new to just about everyone on our team.

Specifically, the game plan called for the plainclothes detective driving the Ryder truck to pull out of the "safe house" and slowly drive along the country roads to the crack cocaine distribution center where he would pull carefully off the roadway onto the grassy lawn between two older wood-frame houses. He would give the "go" order to the detective in the cargo hold, who would swing the rear door open, and half our team (five guys) would exit one side of the van while the other half of the team (now four guys) would exit the other side of the van. Each team would run to the front door of the old houses, conduct the knock and announce, wait for a response to the door and, if no response, hit the door with a large sledgehammer, then enter the house, and secure all occupants. The detectives were arriving on the property almost at the same time, to approach the two mobile homes, to secure the crack cocaine processing centers. The detectives would enter the mobile homes and secure everybody they found inside the operation and secure the evidence which they found inside.

There were other variables involved as during surveillance, the detectives had noted several cars and trucks were always parked on the grounds, with armed bad guys who hung out just watching the property and waiting for product to be brought out. Another purpose of the detectives who followed the Ryder truck to the property was to confront, detain, and handcuff any of the bad guys hanging out in the yard near the vehicles. This would entail securing the bad guys before they could produce any firearms or other weapons to interrupt the SWAT team from their appointed mission.

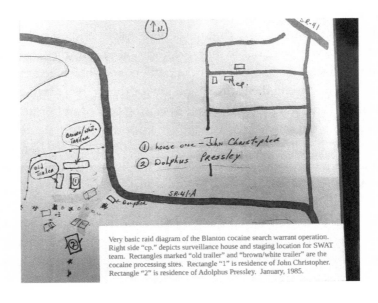

Very basic raid diagram of the Blanton cocaine search warrant operation. Right side "cp." depicts surveillance house and staging location for SWAT team. Rectangles marked "old trailer" and "brown/white trailer" are the cocaine processing sites. Rectangle "1" is residence of John Christopher. Rectangle "2" is residence of Adolphus Pressley. January, 1985.

This seemed like a good game plan to me on the surface based on the minute foundation of tactical information in my developing tactical mindset. But most importantly as a SWAT team, since I joined the team in April 1985, we had not executed a single search warrant. So to say we had no idea how this search warrant operation would end up was a gross understatement. Although there is no possible way I would have bowed out of this operation like "Chicken Little," I completely understood the level of anxiety he must have felt. And as so often occurred during my time in service on the SWAT team, there were times when I had to make my peace with my Lord and Savior, who I prayed to silently and fervently that he guide my actions and guide the aggressive actions of those whom I was about to encounter, to bring justice, to bear peaceably and swiftly, and if this was one of those occasions where I may be in a shooting situation, I prayed the Lord to help me to aim accurately and stop any threats against me or my team or any other innocent persons. If this was my time to be shot, I prayed for life and speedy healing from whatever arms were taken up against me and my team. I prayed for Jesus to be with me since I knew He would protect me and shield me with the Armor of God (Ephesians 6:10).

We finally arrived at the surveillance safe house, where we waited for the cue until we carried all of our weapons and gear out the back of the Ryder truck and rushed into the vacant house to find all the typical stakeout gear and miscellaneous cop equipment laying around. There was a cooler full of bottled water, half-eaten Subway sandwiches, open bags of potato chips, empty Chips Ahoy cookie packages… There were spotting scopes, binoculars, and high-dollar cameras on tripods aimed at the target house. Some of the scopes and binoculars were sitting on the windowsill, which I assumed the detectives had sat before for days on end, watching and documenting the activity at the cocaine distribution center.

Our team members knew the feeling, which we all realized now that we were here. Once we had been to the safe house and saw the inside of their surveillance hideout, the detectives had to go forward with the operation soon. They surely did not want to postpone anything for another day now that we had seen so much of their operation and knew what had been the focus of their investigation for the past two months. Oh! Of course, we all had the common bond of law enforcement, working toward the common goal of arresting drug dealers and putting them behind bars, but we knew too much of this operation to safely watch us go home with the promise we would stay completely quiet and return to carry out their mission tomorrow or another day.

So we found a comfortable spot to lean against a wall and settle down in this vacant empty home to await the next cocaine delivery to the target house. And we waited…

After an afternoon meal of Subway sandwiches, of course, we finally got the word to gear up and prepare to move out. The orders could have just as well been barked out by a drill sergeant wearing a stiff-brimmed round campaign hat to a squad of newly trained army recruits before loading up in their huge diesel transport trucks, then lumbering casually across the army base to begin the journey to a destination where none of them ever expected they would end, while asking, "Is this really happening to me right now?"

CHAPTER 9

MOVE OUT, MOVE OUT, MOVE OUT

And he said: The Lord is my rock and my fortress and my deliverer;
The God of my strength, in whom I will trust; My shield and
the horn of my salvation, My stronghold and my refuge; My
Savior, you save me from violence. I will call upon the Lord, who
is worthy to be praised; So shall I be saved from my enemies.
—2 Samuel 22:2–4

As I carried my shotgun with both hands, safety "on," I waited my turn to round the corner and bolt across the carport to the back of the Ryder truck and climb upon the grated tailgate into the rear cargo hold that finally was packed with nine anxious team members. And of course, the few detectives who had drawn the short straws where they were also relegated to ride in the back of the truck. There just wasn't enough room in the few vehicles driving behind the Ryder Trojan horse truck since a lengthy caravan with a dozen detective vehicles would look quite conspicuous in this neighborhood.

I wondered for a brief moment what type of thoughts went through the minds of the neighbors who had caught a glimpse of our team loading up in the back of the truck before the driver got in, started the engine, and lumbered off toward the search warrant target. I was very certain the locals had not seen this much firepower out here in Blanton in a very long time. But as luck would have it, this event would not be our last SWAT operation in this little country community, but that is another story for another time.

As we lumbered down the bumpy roads that led us to the target, we all tried various handholds, balancing while leaning against the walls while we just tried to keep on our feet until the truck hit those really big bumps as it drove off the road and onto the grass. Suddenly a voice crackled across the radio in our detective's hand, and the voice shouted, "Move out, move out, move out!"

The back door flew up, and the cool fresh evening air hit our faces as our lines began to file out the back of the Ryder truck. With a resounding *click*, my safety moved to the *off* position on my shotgun. I heard voices shouting which I assumed was the detectives confronting the bad guys hanging around the cars in the front of the truck. The sounds were faint as I took off running; the sound of my breathing was heavy in my ears; and my boots moved swiftly across the uneven terrain. I saw the direction our team was heading toward the big two-story ranch house, which loomed up ahead. It looked like a huge formidable target, and I asked myself, "We really are going to search this thing with five guys?"

Unexpectedly, in the corner of my eye, I noticed a tall lanky black male in jeans and a plaid Western shirt as he ran toward the driver's door of a beat-up blue pickup parked thirty yards away in the grassy field. My eyes swept the field ever so quickly, but no one seemed to notice this guy. He continued running toward the truck, and I changed my direction toward the blue pickup as well and screamed as loudly as I could, "Freeze! Right there!"

Just as the man reached the truck door, I leveled the shotgun toward him, my finger curling around the trigger. Screaming a second time, hoping he heard me above the other commotion, "Get down! Get down! Do it now!"

He stopped, let go of the door of the truck, stepped away from the truck, and slowly bent over like an older man might do to carefully get down on all fours. I continued my rant just to make sure he was following my commands, "All the way down! On the ground! Spread your arms and legs! And don't move!"

I could tell now he was looking right at me and following exactly what I was telling him to do. I glanced around quickly, and

Kurt was jogging away from the house, heading across the open yard in front of me.

"Kurt!" I yelled. "I got one down right there," pointing with the Winchester shotgun toward the black male spread out thirty yards downrange.

Kurt yelled back, "Cover me!"

Instinctively, I replied, "Covered," and he ran to the black male, pointing his assault rifle at the man's body as he ran.

Once Kurt had taken a position over the suspect, I stepped around the thick pine trees that I had jumped behind during my commands. I took a quick glance to size them up, and I couldn't help but resist the opportunity to silently compliment myself on my choice of cover. I saw no chance of any bullet penetrating those thick pines while I was giving my commands, then I took off running toward Kurt.

"Coming at ya!" I called, slightly calmer than the earlier yelling I engaged at the suspect. As I pulled up next to Kurt, I announced, "I got cuffs."

He replied, "Got him covered. Cuff him!"

I clicked on the safety of my shotgun, lay it on the ground near me, and pulled my silver metal handcuffs out of my belt, slapping them on the wrists of the suspect while swinging his arms behind his back. Once secured, I told Kurt I had him, and Kurt turned and took off running toward the trailers to finish clearing the other buildings.

I picked up my shotgun and stood over my prisoner while I watched the other activity going on around me. It was then that I heard the team members calling from inside the house. Their voices calm but urgent.

"Little help! We need another SWAT in here!"

I called back, "I hear you. We got suspects covered on the ground."

"Can you break loose?"

"Negative at this time. Stand by a sec."

As I looked for some way to possibly handcuff my suspect to the truck, I stepped over to the truck door, swung the door open just to make sure no one else was hiding inside.

That's when I spotted the gun!

It lay on the seat with the grips angled toward the driver's door for quick and ready access. It looked like a .38 Special or .357 with a six-inch barrel blued coloring but with lots of knicks and scratches all over the finish that made it look like it was probably carried around a lot. Then it hit me. He was going for this gun to start shooting at us. I had a brief picture of the disaster that might have broken loose if he had opened the truck door and grabbed this pistol.

"Hey you!" I said, "is this pistol what you were going for in the truck?"

He rolled his body slightly so he could look up at me with his head while I stood above him pointing my shotgun toward the ground.

"Who ya callin' hey you, boss?" He strained against the hand-cuffs which pinned his arms against his body.

"I'm talking to you." I answered directly.

"Do you know who you're talking to, boss?" He asked me back.

"No, sir. What's your name?" I asked.

"My name is Dolphus Pressley. I am the president of the Pasco Chapter of the NAACP."

Oh…now I remembered. This was the owner of the property. They had covered it in the briefing. They said something about someone here being affiliated with the NAACP. And now here he was, trying to jump in his truck to either grab his gun and start a shootout or drive on out of here. Wow, I thought to myself. My handcuffs were on this guy…and I had had my shotgun pointed at a celebrity who I just ordered to the ground. My day was suddenly looking up.

After the team in the house got some help, the detectives started rounding up the suspects over by the house. I figured I would wait a minute 'til they came over to explain this situation since they would be the ones to originate any charges.

Once the detective came over, I showed him the gun laying "at the ready" on the seat of the beat-up Ford truck.

"He was definitely going for it," I told the heavyset detective wearing the green-and-white windbreaker, identifying him as one of the detectives in this operation.

The detective collected the revolver and the (past) president of the NAACP and walked him over by the rest of the suspects. I was almost done with my role in this raid. All we had to do for the rest of the evening was stand around the suspects and keep an eye on them for security while the detectives went about the task of reading the search warrant, searching everything, and collecting evidence.

Pasco authorities strike suspected cocaine center

This photo caption read: Pasco County detectives take an unidentified man into custody in a raid on a suspected drug operation in Blanton. Tribune photo by Pam Higgins. January, 1985.

As we stood around the entrance of the old wood-framed home, I felt the cool rush of a breeze blow past me, and the beads of sweat streamed down my neck. While my heart rate continued to drop to normal pace again, I thought about the events I had just gone through.

I could've gotten shot if that guy had taken just a few more steps to the door of his truck. I thought about it more as I walked back to the Trojan horse Ryder truck. We all returned back to the original practice site at the fairgrounds, where we peeled off our gear and stashed it away in the trunks of our agency vehicles so we could head home and clean it up 'til the next time we needed it.

That night, of the nine suspects taken into custody, the twenty-six-year-old daughter of Mr. Pressley was charged with possession of cocaine, possession of paraphernalia, and felon in possession of a firearm. The other eight suspects were released after questioning, including Mr. Dolphus Pressley.

And the newspaper report said two days later, "There were no shots fired in the raid."

But no mention was made of how close we came to having a few shots fired, and those shots could have made the difference between any member of our SWAT team or detectives going home that night.

Point taken, sometimes the news or the newspaper story doesn't offer up the whole story. Sometimes there is a lot more to the story than what is printed or how they print it.

As for me and my fellow teammates, we were just glad to be going home that night.

Chapter 10
Barricaded Man in a Van

Blessed is the man who trusts in the Lord, and whose hope
is the Lord. For he shall be like a tree planted by the waters,
which spreads out its roots by the river, and will not fear when
heat comes; But its leaf will be green, and will not be anxious
in the year of drought, nor will cease from yielding fruit.
—Jeremiah 17:7–8

After the raid in January, we had no SWAT calls of any significance, which was a good thing because I was dating a beautiful young dispatcher who I had met through my best friend. We were planning and preparing for a full wedding in later October, until on Tuesday on the week of the wedding, I was working day shift. My mind was already on the festivities, which would begin in just four more days, and the exciting two weeks of vacation honeymoon to follow.

But around 1:00 p.m. on that hot October day, I had stopped off at my doctor's office to have a skin tag checked and burned off my shoulder. I had checked off the radio as out of service, subject to call, while I was in the office, but I didn't expect it to take very long. While I was seated on the examination table, my SWAT pager began beeping incessantly as the doctor was finishing the procedure. The nurse handed it to me just as the doctor finished and stepped away. The nurse applied a gauze dressing and taped it over the small wound on my shoulder.

I saw the phone number for dispatch on the pager, and I asked to use their office phone. The dispatcher advised me to respond over to Gulf Harbors in reference to a barricaded subject, who had an armed confrontation with a deputy before he had retreated into his van. He was still on the scene.

I advised dispatch I was close by, and I could be "97" (on the scene) in just a few minutes. With that, I threw on my vest and uniform shirt and said my quick goodbyes as I headed for my patrol car. Traffic was light for midafternoon as I drove through the streets toward Gulf Harbors, and I thought, *How ironic is this that I stopped off for a quick doctor's visit during my shift, and they get a call of this urgency in my own sector?* In all reality, I felt that I should have been the one responding to the original call, which in all reality was in my sector, Baker 2. As soon as I arrived, I was briefed on the situation. I was assigned to hold a perimeter position on the van to make sure he did not decide to drive off in his van and flee the area.

Much later, I was informed of the background story which led to this barricade, and although the first story I heard was rushed and not completely accurate, I later pieced together all the parts of this "comedy of errors." It seems the suspect, Chester, was separated for a long term from his wife, during which time Chester traveled to Pennsylvania to visit his relatives and friends. During this time, he dated another woman and had an intimate relationship with her, which was never disclosed to his wife in Florida. He had hoped to eventually get back with his wife, but upon his return to Florida, one of his nephews had learned of the romantic fling Uncle Chester had up north and divulged this to Chester's wife.

With that information, Chester's wife filed for divorce and sole custody of Chester's nine-year-old daughter. Chester took up residence with a local woman, and the divorce proceeded without his opportunity to present his side of the story. When Chester discovered the final judgment was entered on October 3, over two weeks prior to the present date, he was very distraught and angry at his nephew who had run his mouth and eliminated all chances of Chester gaining custody of his daughter.

So Chester went on a drinking binge on this day, armed himself with his shotgun, and a .22 caliber revolver, and he went searching for his nephew. Apparently, Chester was going into Gulf Harbors to check the vacant home sites at the far west side of the community since his nephews frequently parked at the vacant lots to fish from the sea walls where they could drop a line into the Gulf waters.

While driving in that direction, Chester came across two of his nephews who had decided to finish up fishing for the day and were leaving. Chester flagged them down, got out of his van with the shotgun, and while aiming at them, he blatantly announced, "You bought the farm!" The nephews responded by quickly backstepping and fast-talking to figure out an escape route. This gave the neighbors time to call the sheriff's office and complain about a loud angry man with a gun in the streets outside their homes.

Overhead view of the SWAT scene in Gulf Harbors, with the white Ford F-150 van in center of the photo. Pasco Sheriff's Office Crime Scene Units are on the scene to conduct the crime scene investigation after the shooting. The cross street in the foreground is Shell Stream Boulevard. Oct. 21, 1986.

When Deputy Rossee showed up on the scene, he was met with a drunk angry Chester armed with a shotgun. Instinctively Rossee scrambled behind his car for cover (a very smart move on his part). During these initial minutes, Chester decided to disengage from arguing with his nephews, and he pulled his van up into a grassy field which was directly alongside Floramar Terrace, the only primary access road leading into and out of Gulf Harbors. To this day, we have never figured out why he chose to merely pull his van out of the street and into this grassy field. However, when Rossee pulled his patrol car into a tactically defensive position to begin to set a perimeter on the van, all traffic entering or leaving Gulf Harbors was blocked off. This all began shortly after 1:00 p.m.

Once the supervisors on duty realized we had a standoff with an armed, barricaded "gunman," they responded to the scene, and more deputies were called to the scene as well. As this standoff wore on, more and more of the midafternoon traffic stacked up on Floramar Terrace, the result of a traffic engineering nightmare with only one access road for the entire community. Soon we had enough deputies on the scene to cover my position, and I was pulled off my perimeter position to meet with the lieutenant in charge, also our SWAT team commander, Lieutenant Weinberg.

The command post was only a small group of patrol vehicles parked in a small group along Floramar Terrace about a hundred yards or so from where Chester sat watching all the commotion from his van. I quickly filled them in on the behaviors I had seen from Chester so far, and tactically I recommended to Lieutenant Weinberg that I deploy into the field on the east side of the van, so I might have a better direct view into the open sliding door of the passenger side of the van. Weinberg quickly agreed, told me to dress out in my SWAT BDUs (battle dress uniform or camouflage fatigues), and get my rifle ready.

I distinctly recall his words about this situation as I pulled my SWAT pants, blouse, and tactical flak vest out of the trunk of my patrol car. He said, "We're gonna talk him out of the van really quick and end this thing as soon as possible."

Well, in the big scheme of things, Weinberg, who had been a member of the SWAT team since its inception in 1979, had much more SWAT knowledge, training, and experience than I did, especially considering he had seven years on the team and about twenty-five SWAT callouts under his belt. My thoughts at the moment were more focused on wrapping up this standoff, finishing my last two days before vacation and getting the last of my wedding preparations done before the *big day* on Saturday! I still had quite a few more errands to run before I watched my new bride walking down the aisle to meet me at the altar. This standoff was just another armed bad guy for our awesome negotiators to talk down from his excited manic emotional state. After which we would safely take him into custody and deliver him to the jail or mental health intake (whichever option they decided).

I looked around for any bystanders watching the events unfold outside their home and quickly picked a nice grandmotherly looking woman standing in her driveway, craning her neck to try to see the deputies down the street from her home. I hustled up her driveway and hurriedly asked if I might borrow her bathroom to change my clothes into a "different" uniform, to which she immediately ushered me into her home to a spare bedroom. I glanced around the bedroom, noticing the lace doilies, porcelain dolls, and knitted afghans on the chair by the bed. I estimated her to be about the same age as my own grandmother who lived on the other side of town. Funny, how the grandparents of that era had such similar taste to create a comfortable environment for a room. I thought for a moment, *What a great place to lay down and take a quick midday nap...if only I had the time.*

Maybe another day. For now, I had a mission, and I was charged with adrenaline to go show my SWAT lieutenant that this SWAT dude, with all of nineteen months on the team, was ready, willing, and able to put in the best effort toward bringing this standoff to a peaceful resolution.

As I left the home of the gracious woman who had just opened her home to me, I jotted down her house number, fully intending to stop back sometime to thank her for allowing me a place to do my uniform change. Even though I had done it before, the front seat of a patrol car was not the easiest place to try to do a quick change into SWAT uniforms. A little privacy was very helpful to me at that moment.

Back at my car, I began quickly loading my equipment onto my duty belt while I pondered how long it had been since I had changed out the water in my OD green plastic canteen. I hoped it was more recently than later.

Deputy Jeff Tanner, gearing up for sniper deployment with Remington .308 sniper rifle. Note revolver in sidearm holster, and no helmet. Oct. 21, 1986.

As I filled my pockets with anything I may need during the course of this assignment, I reflected on the collection of SWAT equipment which I had accumulated in my SWAT bag. It had certainly grown exponentially since a year and a half ago. I flipped open the clips on the side of my hard rifle case and removed my long gun. It was a good specimen of a gun, a Remington .308 caliber rifle with a Redfield three-by-nine sport scope. I had a simple bipod attached to the front of the forestock for extra stability. It was not really intended as a police sniper rifle but more of a hunting rifle, good for hunting deer, wild hog, or other varmints. But I wouldn't know much about that...I had never hunted anything in my life except a good restaurant. Due to the fact the SWAT team didn't have a budget, and all of the equipment purchased thus far in the short seven years of the team's existence had been "mooched" off the patrol budget, the addition of needed SWAT equipment had been an exceptionally slow process. According to the veteran snipers who I had trained with, the hunting rifle which I carried was impounded as evidence in a criminal case years ago, then after the case was closed, it was never claimed. That made it eligible to be converted to the sheriff's office property via court order, and that is how it became one of the two sniper rifles for our team.

I loaded the internal magazine of the rifle with three long gold-colored rifle bullets, and as I inserted the fourth round, I depressed the bullets into the magazine so the bolt could close and lock on the loose round in the chamber. My rifle was now officially "locked and loaded."

I briefly checked with Lieutenant Weinberg to tell him I was ready and moving into position to take up a position east of the van. I confirmed that after I found my best position, I would advise him on the radio of my approximate distance from the "target." With that, I turned to face my adversary who was sitting quietly for a moment in his white Ford Econoline F150 van, probably contemplating his confrontation he just had with his nephews. He probably wondered if this all would make any difference in his plans to try to gain custody of his nine-year-old daughter.

In my tactical way, I walked west on the side of Floramar Terrace about a hundred feet until a large bushy group of trees stood between me and the van, then I cut across the field to the south. I edged closer to the van, then approached the south side of the trees and underbrush. I slung the rifle onto my back, dropped to all fours, and tactically low crawled through the tall grass until I could see just an outline of the van's roof through the upper taller growth of weeds.

As I rooted around in the grass, I searched for somewhat of a clearing where I could lay out prone, keep my rifle supported on its bipod, and try to conserve my energy. As I set up the bipod, I tried to angle the rifle for my best view while still keeping hidden in the tall grass.

I called to Lieutenant Weinberg on the radio, "S-1, in position."

Using my radio designation which meant I was "sniper 1" deployed on this scene, he answered, "10-4, S-1. In position."

I returned, "Distance to target about fifty yards."

"10-4."

Later I would learn my estimate was pretty accurate from the measurements taken by the crime scene investigators when the whole scene was mapped for the investigation. I had been at forty-five yards from Chester, hunkered down in the tall grass, with that midday sun beating down on my dark-green camouflage BDUs. *I was definitely overdressed*, I thought. The only vests which were available for our team had been reappropriated from the military, and they each consisted of two large curved porcelain plates slightly contoured to the shape of a human body. Each front and back plate weighed about twenty pounds and fit tightly inside a heavy-duty canvass carrier which slung over our shoulders and hung down to belt level. I had absolutely no flexibility in the vest, which was never fitted to my body size. So when I lay down prone, looking through my rifle scope, the back of my neck was actually pushing against the back plate at the back panel of the vest as I forced my head up to get a decent view through my rifle scope.

Initially, Chester was very quiet and calm, which was helpful as more team members showed up and deployed onto our perimeter. We had Medfly and Helfrick on the south perimeter, who found their way to a huge load of dirt which had been dumped as if from a dump truck about twenty-five yards due south of the rear of Chester's van. Then there was Sergeant Rock and "Commander" Campbell on north perimeter set up about forty yards to the northeast of Chester's van in a low recess of the ground. They were partially concealed in the tall grass, but they had no cover except for a small wood frame of a bicycle rack.

Soon Sergeant Hennesay joined me in the tall grass on the east side, and we had an effective six-person perimeter formed, with one perimeter point covering Chester with a rifle—me. This was a good perimeter as we only had ten members of the team at that time, and any extra SWAT dudes who arrived could help at the command post if and when they showed up. Or the extra guys could be used to bring food, drink, or supplies out to us in our perimeter positions too if this operation ran long term.

With a solid perimeter in place, we were ready to begin negotiations, but unfortunately, they were still on the way. So my patrol sergeant, Sergeant Jerkins, offered to try to make contact and start the ball rolling. He drove his patrol car around to the south side of the van where he could face the back of the van to call out to Chester. As Sergeant Jerkins began calling, Chester called back, and they began the lengthy push-pull dialogue to try to convince Chester to put down his guns and step out of the van. And we watched Chester, never one to give up anything without getting something in return, tried to bargain for Sergeant Jerkins to take off his gun belt first.

And on it went…the bargaining continued on into the increasingly hot and humid October afternoon as the sweat fell into the tall grass that concealed us while I watched through my magnified view of the rifle scope.

At one point, Chester stepped out of the van, facing directly toward Sergeant Jerkins, challenging him to take off his gun belt. However, the whole time he made this challenge, Chester had propped his shotgun on the bench seat just inside the open side door of the van. Since Sergeant Jerkins was standing twenty-five yards to the rear of the van, he couldn't see the inside of the van or Chester's right hand resting on the shotgun.

I picked up on Chester's little plan and frantically called into the radio. I tried to relay to the command post to tell Sergeant Jerkins how Chester was trying to lure him out to get a shot at him with the shotgun. Sergeant Jerkins wasn't buying it though, and as they debated back and forth, Chester eventually gave up the debate, jumped back in the van, and grabbed his pistol.

As Sergeant Jerkins jumped back behind the patrol car, pistol shots rang out through the air, and Chester had fired wildly into the dirt mound, behind which Medfly and Helfrick were safely hunkered down. I saw the dirt kick up from the dark mound of dirt as I thought, they had surely chosen the best cover out there.

Chester made several more threats to continue his barrage of gunfire, but soon he calmed down and lay down on the floor of the van with his feet propped up on the bench seat.

The drama continued, until I felt like a sports announcer giving the play-by-play calls, alternating between calm periods of rest and smooth dialogue, punctuated by action as Chester grabbed the shotgun or revolver to shoot more rounds at whoever or whatever frustrated him at the moment. Each time he grabbed a gun, Sergeant Hennesay or I announced it quickly over the radio, so everyone could hunker down and brace themselves for the impending blasts. Chester continued this cycle, hyper, and manic, then calm and mellow while the negotiators tried every tactic they could think of to get Chester to surrender.

They staged a mock arrest within his view out the front window of the van, placing his own nephew in handcuffs, then shoving him into the back of a patrol car. But Chester refused to believe his nephew was "really" arrested, so he called their bluff and announced that he didn't believe it.

Next, they brought his brother-in-law up to the street in front of the van so Chester could hear him over the public address speaker. As his brother-in-law pleaded Chester to give up over the blaring speaker, Chester yelled back he didn't believe it was really his brother-in-law talking to him because he couldn't see inside the patrol car. So given that the PA speaker distorted his brother-in-law's voice, there was no way he would give up as per the heartfelt reasonable request.

Another negotiator was brought in now, Sergeant Kinseller. Surely we thought he can get this stubborn, drunk man to give up! And as Kinseller tried everything possible, Chester just continued to resist any and every effort to speak reason and truth to him. Chester stepped out of the van and walked closer to Kinseller 'til he stood near the back tire. They spoke calmly, almost civilly for a while, then Chester turned on his adrenaline again and challenged Kinseller to a fight. Those of us on the perimeter just shook our heads and watched. How could this man honestly believe he could fight his way out of this mess? Then like many who issue a physical challenge, he began to strip off his clothes. First, his plaid dress shirt, T-shirt, and his boots, and as he began to unbuckle his pants, he finally caught the attention of the local residents watching from outside their surrounding homes. As they cheered, seemingly seeing this standoff come to an end, Chester awakened from the intensity of his challenge and jumped back into the van to stop the whole process and interrupt the negotiations once again.

Kinseller dropped his head to wait for Chester to speak to him again. While the sun continued to beat down at the now late-afternoon hour, Sergeant Hennesay and I had grown parched from the intensity and constant narration of the updates to the command post.

Throughout the afternoon, we had watched Chester on a roller coaster of emotions. First, he would work up himself to an agitated anger, often ending up in his flailing the shotgun or pistol around wildly. Sometimes he would fire off a few rounds as if to punctuate his threats with the loud shots. Then he would take a break, usually lying in repose on the floor of the van, resting his feet on the bench seat or transmission cover between the two front seats. This became so predictable, we could anticipate his rant as he grew louder and louder each time.

Then I had a problem. While watching the drama unfold before me, the upper half of the view in my scope began to disappear due to the sun's setting on the horizon on the opposite side of the van. As my scope caught the reflection from the roof of his van, more of my view turned black like an eclipse slowly taking over my scope from top to bottom.

I looked over the field carefully while Chester was laying down at the moment, and I saw some shady ground over to my left near a huge concrete wall that ran the length of the south side of our perimeter. I notified the command post I needed to pull back due to an equipment problem and carefully backed out of my comfortable nest in the tall grass and weeds.

Westward view on Floramar Terrace of Gulf Harbors, depicting the area of the command post and outer perimeter of the incident. Upper right border is the SWAT Command Post vehicle (converted motor home). Oct. 21, 1986.

Pasco Time

When I approached the command post, the crowd along Floramar Terrace had grown exponentially, with a combination of residents trying to get to their homes, and school buses backed up during their appointed rounds, and curious onlookers. Citizens were parked all around the command post, seemingly within dangerously close distances, some of whom were only sixty to seventy yards to the east behind my last position. This put them within only 100–110 yards from Chester's van. When you consider what the army firearms trainers told me years ago, these people were well within range of a stray bullet, which could very well be fatal. I suddenly became very concerned for the vulnerability of this crowd, which had infringed so close to our sacred protected working space at the command post.

I put down my rifle, found a cooler, and discovered it was full of cold-water bottles and Gatorade. It was just what I needed as I made a mental note to myself on the next sniper deployment, I would carry at least a liter of water with me, maybe more.

I guzzled the water and Gatorade until I could drink no more while listening to Lieutenant Weinberg and Captain Bogard discuss the options for replacing me on the sniper position. Bogard looked straight at me and asked, "How are you feeling?"

I replied, "Fine, sir! Just a little hot and sweaty, but once I get some water in me, I'll feel much better."

He followed up, "How long have you been out there?"

I scrunched my face while figuring the time factor as if it was tough to figure out the math when I was this dehydrated. Finally, since I didn't really want to be "benched" from my role in this interesting operation, I grossly underestimated, "Only a few hours."

I tried to figure how much I underestimated that and how believable my estimate was to the captain.

Weinberg called me on it, "Few hours?" As he looked me in the eye, halfway chuckling, Bogard interrupted his funny moment, addressing Weinberg, "Who's your second sniper?"

Lieutenant Weinberg looked at the captain, raised his eyebrows in an obvious are-you-kidding-me look, and in a low voice to express his obvious disagreement at the prospect of playing that card, he said, "It's Commander Campbell."

Bogard looked back at me and abruptly asked, "How long before you can get back out there?"

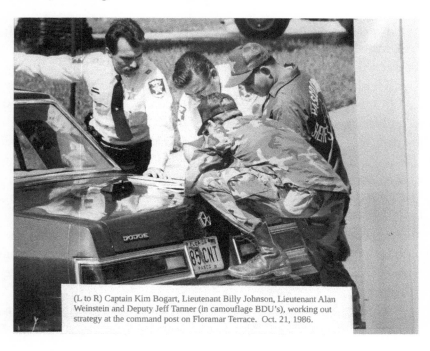

(L to R) Captain Kim Bogart, Lieutenant Billy Johnson, Lieutenant Alan Weinstein and Deputy Jeff Tanner (in camouflage BDU's), working out strategy at the command post on Floramar Terrace. Oct. 21, 1986.

CHAPTER 11
TRYOUTS FOR THE SNIPER TEAM

He gives power to the weak, and to those who have no might He increases strength. Even the youths shall faint and be weary, and the young men shall utterly fall, but those who wait on the Lord shall renew their strength; they shall mount up with wings like eagles, they shall run and not be weary, they shall walk and not faint.
—Isaiah 40:29–31

I knew who the other sniper was for our team as the sniper assignments had not changed much since my appointment to the team. I reflected on the moment when, after attending just a few training days, Deputy Gell announced at that third training day. He said they had approval to expand the sniper unit by two more guys, and they were looking for any members of the team who wanted to "try out" for the positions. As Gell approached and asked if I had ever fired a rifle before, I immediately reflected to Fort Polk and my time spent each Saturday at the rifle club. No one in the group was privy to such knowledge of my past, and I casually answered Gell with a nonchalant, "Yes, sir."

He cocked his head back, squinted his eyes as though to call me out on my abilities as he said, "Good, 'cause we're gonna have some tryouts to see who's the better shot. The winner will make it onto the sniper team."

Inside, I couldn't help but feel a little twinge of excitement. In the few training days thus far, I had seen how dominant the personalities were on this team, and every time they had the opportunity, there was a competition of sorts to declare another alpha male. Although I had not trod on any egos yet, I kept my competitive side hidden, but I really liked this idea of being the "ringer" in this little contest.

So at the next training day, we were getting set up at the Gower's Corner range. Deputy Gell posted some bull's-eye targets downrange, set up his rifle, stepped back, and gestured for me to get into position. As I carefully dropped to "all fours" to adjust the bipod to set the rifle at the best height for me, I slid down into a relaxed prone shooting position. I shifted my head to get a tight cheek weld against the smooth wood stock, taking the crosshairs for a little scan across the target.

After I shifted from one target to the other, I asked, "Which target would you like me to take?"

Kurt answered with a chuckle in his voice, "Whichever one you can hit!"

I smiled slightly, knowingly, while pushing the bolt forward and locking it down into place. I announced calmly, "Ready."

He yelled to all around, "Fire in the hole! Eyes and ears!"

This was the usual announcement for others in the area to get ready for a big bang and make sure you have eye and ear protection in place. The old habits of prone position shooting came right back to me in an instant. Relaxed body, hold the stock tight against the shoulder, firm grip with the trigger hand, adjust the crosshairs onto the bull, breathe slowly but deliberately. Hold the center of the crosshairs on the center of the bull, take a slow full breath, let out a small exhale, crosshairs centered, tighten down the grip while pulling the trigger straight back, and *boom!*

Let the shot surprise you.

That's all there was to it. I unlocked the bolt, ejected the shell, pushed the bolt forward to feed the next round into the chamber, and repeated the process.

After all three .308 rounds were fired at their intended target, I pulled back the bolt, clicked on the safety, and stood up. Kurt was looking me over, smiling slyly.

"Did ya hit anything?" he asked with a wide grin.

I replied knowingly but nonchalantly, "I reckon."

So next up, my buddy, Bobby, who had earned a spot on the team at the same tryout as I lay down at the rifle next. He went through the sequence of firing the three rounds downrange, stood up, and said, "I'm done."

Kurt declared the firing line safe for all, and we walked the fifty yards to the targets. As we got closer, Kurt's expression changed. He looked over at me again. "What target did you shoot again?"

I pointed to the right target. "That one."

The three holes in the center of the bull were combined to form one big hole with three overlapping circles. In shooting circles, they call it a "keyhole shot."

Kurt looked over the target, pulled a quarter out of his pocket, and placed it over the keyhole. He found the quarter covered most of the hole with slivers of daylight shining through at the edges.

I halfway struggled to keep a straight face as if not knowing I had exceeded expectations. Kurt shook his head back and forth one time, raised his eyebrows while looking back at me, and said, "Son! We're gonna make a sniper out of you."

Well, I soon learned what he meant as the role of a sniper is much more than just an accurate marksman with a long gun. Through the next several months, I found myself in some sniper classes where I learned more of the art of taking a concealed position without the intended target detecting any stalking of his position. I practiced sorting through the actions and information produced by suspects when they were in a barricade or hostage situation to relay those actions back to the command post. I learned of the thirteen major mistakes most barricade subjects and hostage takers make when they are in the midst of their high stress operation. And I learned more about the nuances of shooting a high-powered rifle such as the .308 Remington and the .223 M16/AR-15.

I was lucky at the time since our team only had two sniper rifles. The plan for expanding the team involved appointing two new snipers to share the assigned rifles with the current veteran team snipers, to allow the veterans to mentor the rookies, and to deploy as a designated sniper/observer team.

Fortunately, I was assigned to Kurt, while my friend, Bobby, was assigned to Commander Campbell. Lucky for me, Kurt and I could shoot the same rifle without any adjustments to the scope relief, being the distance maintained between the scope and the eye. For shooting a scoped rifle, this was a critical issue, and for that reason, no scope adjustments were required when Kurt and I handed the rifle back and forth.

I listened to much of what Kurt taught me, which along with the skills I had learned in the various seminars, were all valuable skills I had used during the deployment on that October day, although I don't know if anything could have prepared me for the endurance test of holding my concealed position for four hours so far, mostly in the sun, with very little water to sustain me. Yes, this was surely the longest test of my strength, stamina, and endurance to date.

CHAPTER 12
CHESTER'S LAST STAND

Let every soul be subject to the governing authorities. For
there is no authority except from God, and the authorities
that exist are appointed by God. Therefore whoever
resists the authority resists the ordinance of God, and
those who resist will bring judgment on themselves.
—Romans 13:1–2

I abruptly piped up in my defense of returning to the playing field.
"I'm fine," I said. "Just give me a minute to drink some more water,
stretch out a bit, and I'll get back out there."

I continued as if they were going to allow me to redeploy with
no question.

"I had some scope blackout due to the reflection off the top of
the van. If I get into a shaded position, I'll be able to see inside the
van better."

Weinberg looked at Bogard, lifted his bushy black eyebrows in
a "what do you think?" expression. Weinberg glanced at me and said,
"Whenever you can move out, hit it."

I realized I needed to move fast before they changed their minds,
so I took two more swigs of water, stuffed a cold bottle into my pant
leg pocket for later, and slung my rifle over my aching shoulder. I
started off across the extreme east perimeter of the huge field toward
that big concrete wall that ran along the south side. I didn't see any
movement near the van, so I figured I was safe to stay more standing
than crouched since at this point, it was painful to bend over that far.

As I reached the massive concrete wall, I was now far enough south where I could see both Medfly and Helfrick laying behind the huge load of dirt which gave them the best protection ever. I could also see the open side door of the van, although due to the setting sun, the interior of the van already appeared several shades darker, and things seemed more urgent to me. We needed to seek a resolution to this standoff soon, or we were going to be operating in darkness.

I kneeled to take advantage of concealment by the weeds around me and pushed around several of the small mounds of loose dirt and sand which had been packed down by the rain and elements over time. As I opened the bipod and pulled down the legs to give my barrel better elevation, I moved just a bit closer to the van to push down some of the taller grass. I felt some resistance as I pushed the rifle forward, and then abruptly the bipod buckled under the rifle stock. I jerked the rifle back toward me as the bipod broke off the fastener which held it to the forestock of the rifle.

Was it possible for anything else to go wrong today? Just where was "Murphy" today? And why couldn't he find someone else to annoy? I looked over the damage to the bipod attachment piece and quickly thought how I might be able to make the front stock more stable for a precision shot downrange. I noticed at the connection point, where the bipod screwed into the stock, the screw was still attached. That was good to see. I just needed a base to hold the bipod relatively stable, and maybe I could finger tighten the screw into the existing connection.

I had my gas mask in a small canvas bag carrier, strapped around my waist, so I wrapped the waist straps of the carrier around the bag and looped them around the bipod too. This held the carrier to the bipod, and with the connecting hardware halfway fastened to the bipod connection on the stock, I was back in business.

I took a quick swish of water from my extra bottle, glad that I had taken a second to snatch it up before returning to action. Once back in prone position, I gave the command post a confirmation that I was about a hundred yards east of the target. Weinberg confirmed my location, and I took another drink of water. My mind wandered off to several things during this brief break in the action. I thought of the first organ to suffer when the body began to experience dehydration—the eyes. And I thought of the volume of fluids that I had drank so far since I arrived on the scene of this situation—not much. I thought about the hydration lessons learned in sniper class, where you can tell how hydrated you are by the color of your urine. That would work fine if I had drunk enough fluid to go, but in the course of this afternoon, I had not needed to relieve myself.

I thought about the value of our team in responding to take over this barricade, to safely put the time in to allow our many trained and gifted negotiators to speak with Chester to try to talk him into surrendering to us. I thought about the terrible alternatives if we did not even have a SWAT team to spend the time on this situation and if the patrol deputies had to try to resolve this complicated barricade all on their own. I thanked my Lord and Savior that I had drank enough water to keep myself in this operation and my eyes clear enough to focus on my crosshairs and see my target through the scope.

Suddenly Chester came to life again. He began another dialogue with the new negotiator as Kinseller had taken a break or handed the reigns over to another comrade to see if he could get through to Chester. Chester seemed more agitated now like he was pushing for some opportunity to end this test of his patience too.

The command post gave me a call, "CP to S-1."

I answered the call quickly, "S-1, go ahead."

"We are concerned the target may try to go mobile. We have vehicles in position to block him if he takes off… we need to know do you have a clear shot of any of the tires of the van?"

I replied, "S-1. That's 10-4. I can take out the right front tire easiest with the engine block for a backstop so no danger to the bystanders or other perimeter units."

Weinberg came back, "Okay, you have a 'red light' at this time with a conditional green light if he shoots again or tries to go mobile."

I understood the orders and confirmed with the command post while thinking to myself, *If ever this thing comes to an end, I think I'm going to strongly recommend we permanently do away with this "red light, green light" system. It just seemed too difficult to keep track over a long callout, and there seemed too much room for miscommunication and error.*

Throughout the standoff, the command post had constantly changed my permission status to shoot at Chester, where I had no permission to shoot when he was clearly firing his shotgun or revolver at our perimeter men behind the dirt mound. That, in my mind, was clearly an attempted homicide of a law enforcement officer, which was a forcible felony, thus qualified for a shootable offense. As the red-light status changed through the afternoon, I was constantly on watch for any qualifying felonious action which would have justified my shooting Chester to potentially save a life of one of my partners on the perimeter. Although it was not anything I yearned for or wished to happen, I was acutely aware that if Chester should begin shooting again, I may be the only team member in a position to immediately intervene to stop his violence. This was not anything too overwhelming for me to handle, but I took it very seriously. After only a year and a half on the team, I had really felt a close brotherhood with my team members. I did not want our honor guard brothers and sisters to be arranging a law enforcement funeral in the near future.

It was about 5:30 p.m., and Chester wasn't acting so fired up anymore. He sat inside the van, just casually waving the barrel of his shotgun out the side door of the van. He seemed as though he had been empowered beyond measure with an air of superiority after holding off an entire SWAT team for over five hours now.

From their vantage point in front of the van, perimeter members, Sergeant Rock and Commander Campbell, saw the gun barrel extending out the side van door. Campbell decided to make a move as his patience for this marathon was over as well. Campbell told Rock, "Let's start low crawling up to the van, get close to the shotgun, grab it, and take him down."

This decision was not cleared through the command post or passed on to any other team members but more of an individual decision in the heat of the moment. Campbell started crawling forward, and Rock didn't have much choice, so he edged forward too.

As they moved closer, Chester happened to straighten his legs, look out the front windshield of the van, and he spotted the two men in camouflage creeping slowly toward the van. Chester called out to the negotiator frantically as he watched the soon to be intruders coming closer into his territory. He grabbed his shotgun to wave it in the air as if to show everyone he still had a gun, and he wasn't afraid to use it.

The negotiator, confused about the sudden intensity of his tone, called for Chester repeatedly. But Chester was focused on the men in camouflage creeping ever closer.

Chester called out, "Call those guys off! Call them off now, or I'm gonna count to ten and start shooting!"

As Chester called out his threat, I heard it loudly and clearly, even some hundred yards away. But I didn't know if the perimeter units had heard, so I called out on the radio.

"S-1 to perimeter units, he spotted you P-1. Pull back, pull back. He's gonna count to ten and start shooting. Do you copy?"

Campbell came on quickly, "P-1, we read you. We're pulling back."

Weinberg broke through, "P-1, return to cover. Return to cover!"

But it was too late, the damage had been done.

Chester had spotted their advance and felt they were encroaching too close for comfort. He started a countdown from ten loudly for all to hear.

"Ten, nine, eight..."

I watched through the scope as Chester climbed up into the driver's seat of the van to hang out the driver's side window and aim his shotgun in the direction of Rock and Campbell. I realized quickly this was a "green light" action that I was waiting for, but my last instructions were to shoot the tire.

I called a quick warning one more time, "P-1, take cover! Take cover!" Then I started my shooting sequence as he counted, "Five, four, three..."

Anchor that stock in my shoulder, breathing steady, body relaxed, grip that stock with my right hand, cheek weld solid on the buttstock, crosshair on the tire...breathe easy, firm grip with the trigger hand, full breath. I heard the loud *bang* from the shotgun as I had expected.

Briefly I thought about that being the last sound Rock and Campbell heard before buckshot ripped through their bodies. *Crosshair hold on the right front tire of the van, exhale a short breath, hold it now, and press that trigger. Boom!* The .308 exploded with all the fury of a cannon waiting to release its bullet with force and precision. The bullet spiraled off ninety-two yards downrange across the field to the right front tire of the van. It penetrated the tire easily, causing another small explosion as the tire burst, rocking the van.

With that, Medfly and Helfrick fired their tear gas rounds through the glass windows of the rear doors of the van, spewing the rancid smoke in all directions. Quickly they retreated back to the safety of their dirt mound.

I glanced downrange over my scope to see the cloud of smoke which could have been from Chester's shotgun, from the tear gas, and even from the explosion of the .308 bullet penetrating the rubber, inner fender and engine block of the Ford engine. I immediately pulled back the rifle bolt, kicked out the empty shell which flew off to the side in slow motion now. As I started to slide the bolt forward again, it caught against the base of the third round in my magazine, causing a slight jam in the chamber.

I muttered something about "Murphy" again, and the radio crackled to life. It was Campbell… "P-1, P-1, my partner's been hit! My partner's been hit, I need EMS right away!" Lieutenant Weinberg came on, "P-1, confirm! Who's been hit?"

"P-1, Pasco! I need EMS now, Rock's been hit in the head, I need EMS here!"

With that, I knew we had a major problem. It was now an attempted homicide on Sergeant Rock. And if it was a head shot, we could be dealing with a law enforcement homicide now!

I stuck my fingers in the magazine, still in slow motion, just a little bit further now. As I pushed down on bullet #3, I carefully guided the bolt forward to edge bullet #2 slowly into the chamber. Got it!

I locked down the bolt as Lieutenant Weinberg came across the radio.

"C.P. to S-1."

"S-1, go."

"S-1, You have a green light! Repeat, You have a green light!"

"S-1, Copy that!"

My shot preparation kicked in… deep breath, look through the scope, anchor that stock to my shoulder, crosshairs floating over the target. All I could see in the clearing haze was Chester, now on his knees, facing out the open side door. He held the shotgun across his body pointed up toward the roof of the van. With his right hand, he was feeding more shells into the magazine of the gun. His head was looking down at the shotgun which rested diagonally across his body while he loaded it.

The cloud of smoke was already clearing.

I had to pick an aim point, to place my round exactly where I needed it. I carefully centered the horizontal crosshair between the bald spot on top of his head and the round curve of his chin. The center crosshair ran right down the center of his head.

Crosshair fixed, breathe out a little, press the trigger slowly to the rear… Bang!!

The shot ran out but I could barely hear it. I was too focused on holding the rifle tight, hoping my canvas gas mask bag held that bipod in place.

I watched through the scope, as Chester fell to the floor of the van, lifeless and the shotgun fell out the side door. I had followed the bullet through the scope all the way to the target. Just like in training.

I picked up my radio. "S-1 to C.P. I took the shot. Be advised, subject is down. I repeat, subject is motionless at this time."

Lieutenant Weinberg came back.

"C.P. to P-2. C.P. to P-2. Can you approach the van and check suspect's status?"

P-2 responded, "That's 10-4 command post. Give us a minute to put on our gas masks." With that, Medfly and Helfrick pulled their masks on and Hennesay from my original P-1 position donned his gas mask and they took up arms, carefully pointed at the van. They stepped carefully around the dirt mound and advanced toward the van until they could see into the darkening interior. The setting sun was dropping further below the horizon, and our light was giving way to more and more darkness, especially inside of the van.

As Medfly, Helfrick and Hennesay reached the van, someone reached inside to check the body. But Chester didn't move. He had finally finished his protest, his angry rant, his last stand.

Medfly broke the silence, "P-2 to C.P. P-2 to C.P. Subject is signal 7."

A SWAT perimeter member advanced to check the status of the suspect, Chester Wisneski after he had been fatally shot by Deputy Jeff Tanner while barricaded inside of the white Ford F-150 van for five hours. Note the perimeter units to the south of the van had just fired tear gas rounds with their shotgun through the rear window of the van, when Wisneski fired his shotgun at Sgt. Skip Stone. Hence the need for the SWAT member wearing a gas mask while approaching the van. Oct. 21, 1986.

As they announced the universal code for "dead body" everyone within earshot of our radios knew that meant Chester was dead. And as the C.P. came back on the air to announce that E.M.S. was coming into the scene to get Sergeant Rock, we all turned our attention to him, and his condition.

Pasco Times — JIM STEM

Sgt. Skip Stone has blood on his face after being grazed by a bullet when the SWAT team charged the van.

After being struck with a birdshot pellet, lodged under his scalp, Sgt. Stone unloaded his shotgun prior to his trip to the local hospital emergency room to have the pellet removed and staples applied. Oct. 21, 1986.

We listened intently to the radio for any word of his condition. But even the update that the ambulance was going over to treat him was good news.

I felt a sense of overwhelming relief wash over me. I was initially thankful that this stressful, intense standoff was over, but sorrowful that it ended the way it did. I gathered some of my equipment from the ground around my shooting position, and found a scrap piece of white PVC piping to plant into the sandy hill where I had lain. I placed it firmly so the crime scene investigators could use it to measure the distance of the shot, for the later preparation of the crime scene diagram.

I recalled the universal assessment of a successful SWAT operation. From the SWAT sniper training, they had told me the measure of a successful SWAT operation is one where nobody is injured, killed, and everyone goes home or the bad guy goes to jail or mental health assessment center, etc. Well, I thought to myself, I guess this one wasn't a success.

I slowly got to my feet, happy that I didn't have to low crawl back to the command post. I stretched and felt the aches and pains shoot across my back, neck and shoulders. I pulled out my bottle of water, splashed the parched part in the back of my mouth and picked up my rifle.

I left the two remaining rounds in the rifle magazine, for crime scene documentation, picked up my two empty shells and put them in my pocket. I unwrapped my gas mask bag from the bipod and thought to myself, I hope I never have to count on that for a shooting base again.

As I turned around, there was Helfrick, standing in front of me. He patted me on the back and asked how I was, as though we hadn't spoken in a long time. I told him I was fine, but the guy in the van might need some help. It was that dark humor, trying to make light of the gravity of this situation before us. I guess I just didn't expect it so soon.

Those deep, dark, emotional moments that cops have such a hard time speaking about, always get covered with the morbid jokes, the laughter, whatever it took to keep it lighter.

I asked, "How's Rock?"

Helfrick answered, "He's gonna be OK. He was walking to the ambulance, still bleeding where he got hit in the top of the head."

He explained, as Chester counted down, Rock and Campbell had crawled backwards as far as they could, then they just put their heads down and waited. So with Rock's head being so big, it was the only thing to catch a pellet from Chester's bird shot!

Amazingly, Chester was shooting his shotgun with bird shot.

Helfrick and I began walking off toward the command post, when Helfrick asked, "Do you want to go have a look?"

"Look at Chester?" I asked.

"Yeah! Don't you want to see where you hit him?"

I realized he didn't know that I had watched the shot, to the target. I could tell him where I put that bullet, but I wasn't going to sound cocky at that moment. I had too much respect for Helfrick.

"No, thanks." "I'm good." I continued, "Just ready to get out of this vest."

Helfrick walked with me across the field, complimenting me on the shot from a distance, later determined to be ninety-two yards. I thanked him, and added, I was just happy I could get the shot off to keep Chester from shooting anybody else. And, I was.

As we arrived at our cars, I walked to the trunk, opened the rifle case and gently lay my rifle in the foam cushion. I reached into my pockets for the extra box of ammo, and stashed my equipment in the SWAT bag in my trunk. It was a mess now, like it usually was after a SWAT callout.

As I finally lifted the heavy vest over my head, the October air seemed to be cooling off just a bit. I let out a deep breath and closed my eyes for a few seconds.

Wow! I had just taken a life out there on the battlefield, only minutes ago. So I had just answered that one critical question most cops begin to contemplate when they go through basic firearms training in the police academy. If I need to pull the trigger to stop a deadly threat, can I do it?

How many times had I asked myself that question? How many times had I heard other deputies talking about it?... or bragging about how they would do it without any hesitation or second thought. How many times did I hear the talk in the patrol room, deputies second-guessing their street partners over shooting someone with a knife, a box cutter, an old, rusted, antique looking gun?

Yes, I had heard it all the time. But now, I wondered if I would be the topic of those same chats around the patrol room. It seemed inevitable but I wasn't worried. I thought about all the many times Chester was firing wildly at my partners, yet I had held my fire under the restriction of that stupid "Red Light." If we didn't have to follow the command post restrictions, I could have kept Rock from getting hit. Chester would have been taken out of the equation much earlier, with no opportunity to shoot any team members.

I opened my eyes abruptly and looked around. The big motor home painted in green and white as our mobile command post had been brought to the scene and was now parked alongside Floramar Terrace. I walked over to the door, opened it to feel the cool wave of air conditioning wash over me. I stepped inside. Someone tossed me a cold water and I took a long guzzle as the team members offered their congratulations on my long distant shot to end this marathon.

We chatted while the rooftop air conditioning unit hummed along and everyone offered their observations about the stand-off. We talked about how we handled it with the minimal SWAT personnel needed, when Pinellas or Hillsborough County would have needed at least twenty- to twenty-five team members, two sniper/observer units, a bomb squad, two K-9 teams and an air unit.

We all laughed, as that was the easiest way at the moment to release the pent up stress we were all feeling. The remainder of the evening was spent back at the office, where we took turns meeting with the homicide detectives, going into the deposition in the Sheriff's conference room where the State Attorney asked us specific questions and our testimony was forever preserved by the court reporter who copied our testimony word for word.

I sat quietly in the offices of the Property Crimes detectives, jotting down detailed notes for later transfer into my written report. As the fatigue began to take hold, Det. Wilber came in and asked me where my rifle was. I told him it was still locked in my trunk, but if he was ready, I could turn it over to him now.

He said he was ready, and we walked out to my car, opened the trunk and I took it out. I went through the process of opening the bolt, so he could see it was clear, and the internal magazine still held the two remaining bullets. I took them out and handed them over to him. Det. Wilbur placed them in a paper evidence bag, scribbled on the bag for later reference. I took out the two spent shell casings from my pocket and dropped them into another evidence bag for him. Det. Wilbur scribbled on that bag too, and as I secured my rifle back inside the hard case, I locked the side clips. We chatted about the incident. I was happy that so many people, especially this senior detective who was so highly respected in the agency had many compliments for me on the efforts and professionalism of our SWAT Team. I sincerely appreciated the time he spent to put me at ease, especially at this time when I turned over my rifle, live rounds and spent rounds, to be placed into evidence. This was the point when I realized, technically I was the "suspect" in this case which would be labeled a "homicide."

I understood this entire case would go to the State Attorney of our 6th Judicial Circuit after all the investigations were completed and the depositions were transcribed.

All I wanted to do at this point was go home and soak in a hot bath!

Thankfully, that was my next move, and they allowed me to leave the office and go home, get some rest, and come back the next day to dictate my report. I couldn't get out of there quickly enough. And that hot bath felt so good once I finally stepped into the sudsy water. The hour of relaxation was a long time coming for my tight muscles.

Four days later, I watched my lovely bride walk down the aisle. We said our vows to each other, exchanged rings and pledged our love. I thought it was perfect, and she did as well.

After a week at a beautiful condo in Daytona Beach, and playing tourist at many exciting places in central Florida, I packed up and traveled to Orlando to participate in a week of SWAT training exercises, classes and competition at the International SWAT Round-up Events, hosted annually by the Orlando Police Department, Orange County Sheriff's Office and several surrounding agencies. Our six-person team had the good fortune to enter into five highly competitive events against SWAT Teams from all over the United States, as well as several foreign countries too.

We had a great time and didn't do too badly in our competitive events either. We learned many good things from the educational training classes, and upon returning to Pasco, we formulated some effective strategies for how we could do even better next year. Given our success at the SWAT Round-up, following this late October barricaded suspect operation, our team had made significant progress toward achieving a higher level of professionalism. This seemed to boost the level of pride among all our team members as we enjoyed a history of success and a good reputation within our agency.

I can sum up the pride that I felt when I showed up at the next scheduled SWAT training day, and Lieutenant Weinberg walked up to me before we began the training. He looked me in the eyes, seemingly fumbling for the right words. He said to me after a shooting like I had been through, many guys would consider quitting the team. He explained how many SWAT guys would need to work through some things and "deal" with the shooting, which I was free to do if I needed to take some time off.

I looked him in the eye, strong in my conviction and strong in my word. "I'm staying on the team," I said. "This is my team!"

CHAPTER 13
THE FOLLOWING YEARS

But as it is written: "Eye has not seen, nor ear heard,
nor have entered into the heart of man the things which
God has prepared for those who love Him." But God
has revealed them to us through His Spirit. For the Spirit
searches all things, yes, the deep things of God.
—1 Corinthians 2:9–10

As history played out, I did stay on that team. I served two years on the sniper team followed by five more years as the lead sniper. Then through a fortunate series of promotions, after I had been promoted to sergeant on June 1, 1992, I was appointed SWAT team commander for eight years. My last year as the SWAT commander was spent training then Lieutenant Rock as my successor SWAT commander.

At that point, due to a conflict with the operation's major who had an issue with my resolution of a hostage situation, I decided to leave the team for a year.

However, when a new sheriff was elected in 2000, my team pushed the new team commander to bring me back on the team. I returned to the team in January 2001 as a team leader. I enjoyed this position so much I stayed for ten years, finally retiring from the team in January 2011.

All in all, I enjoyed twenty-five years of service on our team. This was a team longevity record at the time of my resignation from the team of which I was very proud.

After the Gulf Harbors shooting, our core team held
for many more years on search warrants, arrest warrants, barri
situations, hostage situations, and dignitary protection requests.
Many more dangerous encounters were faced by every member of
our team, but with blessings and a hedge of protection, our team
survived with only occasional injuries.

A change of culture on our team occurred after a search warrant on a drug house on September 12, 2002, in which the suspect
shot one of our team members in the head. The bullet, fortunately
only a small .32 caliber round, struck the front edge of his helmet,
broke apart, and sent fragments into his face. He survived, and upon
returning to active duty, he returned to our team with a renewed
faith which spread like wildfire to the rest of our team.

Following this shooting, Gordy began printing up copies of
a verse from Ephesians 6:10, referencing "The Armor of God." I
would strongly encourage anyone reading this who works in a dangerous line of work to open your Bible and read and dwell upon
"The Armor of God" from Ephesians 6:10 to the end of the chapter.
You should pray for the Lord to cover you with the Armor of God.

During a SWAT Round-up competition in Orlando, Florida,
merely two months after that search warrant, Gordy was handing out
hundreds of the laminated verses of "The Armor of God" to any and
every SWAT member who would take one. Gordy was rock-solid in
his faith as surely everyone would expect after having been through
an experience such as his. I have never been shot, let alone shot in
the face like my good friend, Gordy. But to survive such a traumatic
event and then turn around to use it to spread evangelism to other
SWAT members and people from throughout the United States and
abroad was truly a wonderful thing to watch.

Even better, at the next search warrant for our team with Gordy
on board the van, we paused while en route to the target location
while Gordy offered a prayer. He praised God for the blessings in our
lives; he prayed for the "subjects" who were at the search warrant that
they would not take up arms against us; and then he prayed that if
the other parties took up arms that our reaction would be swift, sure,
and effective to eliminate any threats brought against us, to eliminate

the fiery darts of the enemy. He prayed that Jesus be with us all and keep us safe through the entire operation and deliver us safely to our families after we were done.

This prayer became the norm for our team while en route to every search warrant during our ride in the command post van or whatever vehicle we were using for transport. And if for some reason Gordy was not able to join us on a mission, I would say the prayer, or one of the other team leaders would say it.

Everyone on the team realized just how fragile our lives were and how we could lose a teammate so easily. It was a higher priority to take every precaution to employ our faith, to keep every advantage in our favor. If stacking the deck in our favor meant calling upon our God, we did it with no reservations. We all knew our God is an awesome God, and with Him, anything truly is possible.

"I can do all things through Christ who strengthens me" (Philippians 4:13).

Finally, this may surprise you, but for so many years while serving on the SWAT team and in my regular duties at the sheriff's office, I risked my life time and again without truly knowing that I know that I know that I know, that if I died in line of duty, I would go to heaven. That is until June 2002 when I was going through a divorce, and I found myself in a church service at Calvary Chapel Worship Service in New Port Richey. Pastor Bill Strayer was preaching on hitting "rock bottom" and the difficulties which you face when trying to get up again and move forward when you are in the worst possible place. I listened during the service, then following the service, with tears streaming down my face, I knew Pastor Strayer was speaking straight to my heart. I prayed the sinners' prayer with Pastor Strayer to accept Jesus Christ as my Lord and Savior.

If you don't know what the Bible says about being saved, the following verses will explain it more thoroughly:

> Truly, truly, I say to you, unless one is born again,
> he cannot see the Kingdom of God. (John 3:3)

And everyone who calls on the name of the Lord will be saved. (Acts 2:21)

If you confess with your mouth, "Jesus is Lord," and believe in your heart that God raised Him from the dead, you will be saved. For it is with your heart that you believe and are justified, and it is with your mouth that you confess and are saved. (Romans 10:9–10)

For it is by grace you have been saved, through faith and this is not from yourselves. It is the gift of God and not by works, so that no one can boast. (Ephesians 2:8–9)

If you pray this prayer of salvation, Jesus will come right into your heart; you become a Christian; and you will go to heaven when you die and live forever.

Lord Jesus, I have sinned against You in many ways. I believe You died on the cross for my sins and rose from the dead. Forgive me of all my sins and give me the gift of eternal life. Come into my life as Savior and Lord. Help me become the person You want me to be. Amen.

Now you are on your way. The next steps are easy. Just find a good Christian church that teaches sound Christian doctrine, attend so you can meet other supportive Christians, pray to our God and Jesus regularly, read His Word as it is truly the bread of life, and you have begun your Christian walk.

For further guidance, speak to your pastor, and he/she will certainly be glad to mentor you.

And that, my dear friend is the beginning of your journey to developing your SWAT mentality.

I wish you safe travels in your journey and all of God's blessings.

About the Author

Jeff Tanner retired from the Pasco Sheriff's Office as a sergeant in 2013 after thirty years of dedicated service to the citizens of Pasco County, Florida. During his time in service, he served twenty-five years on the agency SWAT team in the roles of sniper, team commander, and finally as team leader. His SWAT team service provided the foundation for the tactical concepts discussed in this book, combined with his personal experiences while growing up, psychological education, and strong Christian maturity. Jeff has pursued a role in the Florida medical marijuana industry over the past six years, which led him to work various security operations in Colorado, attending educational seminars and joining a founders' group of a Florida cannabis business.

Jeff currently enjoys living in St. Augustine, Florida, where he serves at Good News Church. He spends his spare time riding his bikes (on roads, trails, and beaches), target shooting, and reading.

CPSIA information can be obtained
at www.ICGtesting.com
Printed in the USA
LVHW091626300520
657026LV00001B/152